An
Attitude
of
Expectancy

Our Choices Control Our Existence

Mary E. Banks

www.trafford.com
North America & international
toll-free: 1 888 232 4444 (USA & Canada)
fax: 812 355 4082

MARY BANKS' book is part memoir and part testimonial-tips based on her years of journaling life events. The book is filled with many experiences. It is also filled with stories that her relatives told her as a young girl.

Her hope is that this book will allow people to know that they are not alone. It is her prayer that people will learn to never give up. She wants people to continue to strive for the very best.

Mary wants people to know that success is not the size of your house, car or closets. It is not about how much money that you have in your bank account. Success is about relationships. She encourages everyone to look to the *Word* and not the world. You can have great things but in order to keep what God gives you depends on your true relationship with Him.

She encourages people to see themselves the way that God does and to always remember to go to God. He is the one who has strategic instructions for all of those who believe.

TABLE OF CONTENTS

INTRODUCTION

We all have one thing in common. We are all trying to live the best life we know how to live. We are trying our best to make each day better. If you are stuck on pause and caught between two options, pray about it and make your transition. Slide right into your purpose.

There are many things that you will find out in life, whether you grew up on a farm, a trailer park or the projects. You may even have been raised in a middle class environment, a group home, foster care, juvenile detention or perhaps in an upper class lifestyle. Regardless of where you came from, you will discover that no one will ever love you the way that you can. You must take care of you.

If money was plentiful, you learned that money can't buy you happiness. Happiness comes from within. In life, we create our own happiness. The older we get, we find out that the people around us are simply a bonus. There is not one person on this earth who can complete us. We complete ourselves and allow the people around us to join in our wholeness. If we are missing anything, we must work on that void in order to prevent any future disappointment in relationships.

Each day we get older. As we get older, we wake up and discover that skin and hair changes. You wake up one day and discover that this wasn't here yesterday. Not only does our bodies change daily, but our thinking also changes. If there is one mistake that continues to follow you; ask God for correction and just keep it moving. If there are restrictions because of mistakes that were made, try to deal with them in an honest fashion and forgive. Many people believe that forgiveness is just for the other person. Forgiveness is not just for the other person but it is for you. If you don't believe me, take the following test. Think about the days you've wasted pondering over those whom you do not forgive. Go down the list of details that led to the problem and examine just how you felt after putting yourself threw such an ordeal.

Next, take a few days cleansing your mind of every thought that is negative. Go down the list of people who have hurt you and forgive them. Tell yourself that you forgive them and that you want a clear conscience from any negativity. Once you have done this, your very own life becomes peaceful and happy. This takes practice when you consistently go through trials.

The truth is that love and forgiveness allow us to live longer and happier lives. You may not be able to live the rest of your life around certain people, but at least you tried and at least you forgave.

Journal your thoughts as a way of support for separating the negativity away from you; and tell yourself, "I forgive." Say it continuously until it is not an issue anymore. The mind needs a positive anchor in order to gain closure. If we cannot ignore critics, it's like remaining in a comatose state of mind. The mind needs closure from deep-seated pain and emotional betrayal.

Remember that you are not the only person that they would have hurt. They would have done that to somebody else. Fear and un-forgiveness are like locked doors. Fear clouds the truth.

FORGIVENESS IS *YOUR* GIFT

Some people will never change. We don't have a right to change anyone or to force a change on anyone. Don't take it personal. We must work on being responsible for what we say and not what people understand. The minute you forgive, you will find a peace that passes all understanding. Your world changes when you forgive others.

We all know someone who behaves unkindly because something happened to them. They constantly push all blame on others. There are people who cannot love everybody around them at the same time.

Someone asked me does God really exist? We grow up hearing and learning about God. As we grow older, we become our own decision makers. How can you get to know anybody without spending time around them? The same applies to God. If you spend time with God, you will find out about Him. We need God to get us through those tough circumstances. We also need Him when things are good.

I grew up in low income housing. I remember my dad being home but eventually we were raised by our mother. Mom and dad simply did not get along. One day mom called our uncle Steve. She instructed him not to tell anyone about the changes that she was about to make in our household. My uncle wasn't working and had been living with my grandmother. Our grandfather had passed away. My uncle walked from my grandmother's house to our 3 bedroom townhouse in the projects. This was a 10 mile walk in the middle of the night. I had four blood brothers at this time. Later, when we all grew up, mom adopted 2 girls and a boy.

Growing up in the townhouse, mom had her own bedroom. I had my own bedroom and my four brothers shared a room. The boy's room contained two sets of bunk beds. My uncle monitored every move we made and my mom began to work. Later, I remember scheduling visits and lunches with dad. We were never allowed to say one negative word about dad. After his absence from the house, there was a quiet, spirit of peace in the house. Our uncle became a live-in nanny. He cooked, cleaned, did the laundry, ironed and walked us to school. Uncle Steve was very funny and joked most of the time.

THE BEST POT OF CHILI

Once, he made the best pot of chili out of pork and beans. I loved "I Spy," the detective show. The only problem was that it came on late at night and I would be sleep and had school the next morning. Uncle Steve would wake me up to watch the show. There would be a fresh bowl of popcorn in front of the living room's black and white television. I didn't know what microwave popcorn was back then. I was a human remote control. I turned the channel when grownups asked. In the "Mr. Clean" commercials, he seemed to have a very dark tan with the largest hoop earring that I ever saw. All of the commercials were cartoons. The TV was small, but I thought the TV was 10 feet tall. As soon as the show ended, my uncle would say, "Alright Marilyn, back to bed." And off I went. I didn't see the show often but when I could, I was happy. Uncle Steve never called me "Mary," it was always "Marilyn." My mom called me "Duchess" and sometimes "Peaches" back then.

Eventually mom moved and turned her house into a safe haven for foster children. When DCFS needed emergency shelter for children who were taken out of their homes in the middle of the night, the authorities sent them to my mom. Mom would keep them until the next day. Some children stayed for weeks or even months. Later she adopted a few.

This was her ministry. She helped so many children. She raised her own children and so many others. Mom taught all of us how to drive.

She also taught us lots of life's lessons that I pass down to my own. One of the best lessons that I can remember is to always remain close to your siblings. My oldest brother kind of took over after our uncle. Mom worked at Spiegel's and Hearthside Nursing Home. My big brother cleaned the house and made us do our homework. For some reason we would take a knife and clean the corners out of the rooms before waxing floors. We would strip the wax off the floors before re-applying another coat. My mom was super clean and had all white furniture and white carpet with 5 small children.

When we all began to get older, my big brother liked to fight; and he would even fight me. Eventually mom stopped working and became a stay-at-home mom. One thing that I learned from my big brother was how to fight. I can't remember getting bullied too much. I was quiet as a young girl and some classmates would ball up their fist, point to their eyes, hinting about a black eye. Then they would say, "3:15." That meant, after school you were getting beat up. Well,

I had the kind of mother that if you came home and allowed someone to beat you up, she'd get you too. Our childhoods have so much to do with how we turn out as adults.

I was more afraid of my mother and I was pretty good at defending myself. Later, I discovered that my brothers were following and watching me walk home so many times.

They were protecting me without me even knowing that they were watching me. It is kind of how God protects us. You may not see Him but He's watching over us. Charlotte was the girl that I would fight the most. Most of our fights were instigated by the other girls at school. One day our moms got together to talk. Her mom eventually sent for me and put me in her pom-pom girl's squad along with Charlotte. I was in the Bud Billiken parade 4 years straight. At home, if any of us were not speaking to each other; mom made us spend the entire day together until we made up. We were sent to the store together or made to clean the kitchen together. We also had to do homework together. Whatever it took, she made us close. We would try to out-smart mom by not allowing her to know things.

We knew that she would make us partner in everything for that day. Mom had radar and she knew everything. She would call us together and say, "Alright, what's going on?" "You two aren't speaking to each other."

We never got away with ignoring each other. As adults, I am close to all of my siblings. My family conquered many challenges in life. Today all of us are saved. Now that's a blessing. Our generation dealt with things. Even the neighbors put you in your place if necessary.

CHICAGO BLIZZARD

Take your memories and write them down. Remember who you are and where you came from in life. In 1967, I remember a snow fall. The snow was so high. I remember running outside into the snow for fun with no boots and I lost my shoe. I remember thinking that once all of the snow melted I would get my favorite shoe back. I never saw it again. During that winter, we got 23" of snow and later that snow was known as the Chicago Blizzard of 1967. It was record setting. I was very small but there are a lot of things that I do remember about my childhood. Helicopters delivered emergency food during the Chicago blizzard. In 1969, I entered kindergarten. Mrs. Bradley was my teacher and her husband was the principal. Mrs. Bradley was an African American woman. She was so pretty and wore her hair in a perfectly neat bun. Her dresses were worn to perfection. She was well-versed and spoke with the most exquisite tone. Her words were polished and she expected nothing less from her students.

Young ladies were not to enter her classroom wearing pants. When it was cold outside, her girls wore stirrups underneath the skirts. There was a parlor before you entered her classroom. The girls quietly slipped off their stirrup pants and hung them on the hook. Everyone wore skirts with tights. You could hear a pin drop in Mrs. Bradley's class and even in the halls of our school.

ELEMENTARY SCHOOL REUNION

There was prayer in school at this time. Carver Primary School was unique. When the lunches were delivered, the children would call the sandwiches "chokies." Mrs. Bradley would ask daily for our class to return our sandwiches. Some days we were hungry and didn't want to give that cold sandwich back, but you never disrespected the teacher.

Mrs. Bradley felt that the sandwiches weren't fresh or healthy enough for her students and never allowed us to have them. Every day we each got fresh baked cookies from a bakery that she frequented. We would get two large fresh cookies and had them with milk and fruit. Later we took a nap by laying our heads quietly on the top of our desks as Mrs. Bradley prepared our homework assignments. We lined up in the halls. Our lines were straight and even washroom breaks were quiet and orderly. My first grade teacher was Ms. Fields. We went to her home for barbeques after field trips. We were her children. Our class met the Mayor of Gary, Indiana, and visited Operation PUSH events. Ms. Fields managed to keep the same students through my 1st, 2nd, and 3rd grades. Forty years later, Dr. Fields gave us an elementary school reunion. This was held at a hotel banquet facility in Alsip, Illinois. We did a tribute to the students who passed. I facilitated that part of the reunion. The table center pieces were surrounded with photos of us sitting in her classrooms in the 1970s. There were even photos of our fieldtrips.

Any one of us who had returned to college or who had children in school received a gift. The gift was a packet filled with school supplies.

Next, we were called to the podium one by one. We each received a packet filled with assignments, drawings and scripts from plays that Dr. Fields kept for the past 40 years. I was the only one still living in Chicago.

Mary speaking at her elementary school class reunion

We gave Dr. Fields gifts which included an afghan with photos of her students woven inside of the blanket. Then we gave her a souvenir book that was personalized. Everything about this reunion was unique and special. Dr. Fields lives in Georgia and visits my home when she's in town. The most special visit to me was when she came over and helped my daughter, Jessica with her homework. It is not often that a person can say that their first grade teacher came over and helped their child with homework. I also attended my 30 year high school class reunion.

Currently, I am in touch with many of my former classmates. It is so good to get together with old classmates. We also celebrate special occasions together.

Altgeld Gardens is a Chicago Housing Authority located on the far south side of Chicago. It was built in 1944. It was primarily built for the needs of African American veterans returning from World War II. Initially it was owned by the federal government but later granted to the CHA in 1956.

It is named after John Peter Altgeld, an Illinois governor in the 1890s. It is a historic landmark since it is one of the first public housing developments ever built in the United States. There were beautiful flower gardens everywhere. Growing up there, everyone knew each other. My dentist was a young African American lady. She always appeared pleasant and one day she sat me down and talked to me about brushing a better way. She said, "If you don't take care of your teeth, boys won't like you when you get older." She was so pretty and had pearly white teeth with long hair.

Altgeld Garden's flower gardens extended for blocks

Today, I take excellent care of my smile because it is the healthy thing to do.

Everyone in the community used the same doctor. In the old neighborhood everything was convenient. The drug store, grocery store, shoe shop, currency exchange, etc all sat on the same block. Everyone came outside to play at the same time. We all played softball, jump-rope, basketball, ice hockey and hopscotch.

My brothers are the best ice hockey players. I was an excellent ice skater. Before the street lights came on, the entire block of children began to run because we all knew that it was dinner time and you were never caught outside after the street lights. Everybody ate dinner at the table together.

BLACK PANTHERS

Each household was addressed by their last names. They would say, "The Sykes" from block 7, or "The Trotters" etc. There were mixed races in the neighborhood back in the 1970s and the doctors made house-calls. I also can remember the milk man delivering the milk to the back porch. I would sit the empty milk bottle back inside of the cart for him to retrieve when he returned with fresh milk.

Eventually we began to receive hot lunches at school. The black panthers raised money and made sure that we received free hot meals at school. We also received other medical services. The panthers were very serious.

Once I can remember the men standing outside discussing how the panthers needed more members. They said that recruitment was going on this particular day. All of the men sent the women and children inside of their homes and the men waited outside.

The men stood in the middle of the streets. There were crowds of angry men everywhere. They wrote on the ground near the entrance to our neighborhood, "RIGHT HERE HUEY!" They wrote it with white chalk in bold letters. The women refused to stay inside. They joined the men. They stood outside until it got dark and no one ever showed. Nothing was ever spoken about that situation again; at least not in front of me.

I liked going to "Sock hops." Sock hops were high school parties held in the gymnasium.

You removed your shoes and danced in your socks. My mom didn't allow me to attend many house parties but she didn't have a problem with the school parties. When I did attend the house parties my brothers and their friends were right there.

Once, I allowed a guy to slow dance with me. I was dancing with my eyes closed and when I opened my eyes, and while still dancing; one of my brother's friends was looking so closely in my face. He was so close that our noses could touch. I got so angry that I went home. My brothers and their friends would look like, mission accomplished. Our house was the house that all of the children played and all of the guys on that block felt that I was their little sister. I didn't like it when they got overly protective. Many times during the 1980s, I often walked with a limp. This usually happened when it got cold outside. It felt as though my bones would ache. Some mornings I would walk to school with no problem. But there were days when I could not walk. Sometimes I'd make it to school and could not walk back home. For some reason I would make it to a certain tree stump near a set of railroad tracks. I'd sit there until I could walk again.

HIGH SCHOOL & PROM

I would rub my legs with oils, wrap up in leg warmers and pray. I didn't understand why I had to hurt so badly. It was so painful to crawl down on my knees to pray. I was desperate. I wish that I could remember the day that the pain left but I do not. One day God healed me and the pain left for good. Prayer works!

High school was fun in so many ways. I ran for senior class president. Even though I lost, the experience was educational. Since I lost by only a few votes, they asked me to be a class representative. My artwork and paintings were displayed in my high school corridors.

Art plays an important role in life. It fits in the way you decorate and plan recreation. I played the flute in my high school marching band and jazz band. I always dreamt of going on the prom.

When I arrived to school at the beginning of my senior year, a few boys asked me to go. I told each of them that I would let them know. I found myself arguing with them about colors or the most simplest things. I was working at the neighborhood community center at the time.

One day, mom called me at work. I was disappointed because mom was trying to talk me into going to prom with one of my brothers. Finally my mom called and said, "Do you know a boy named Jim?" I said "Yes," he is in the Navy. She went on to say that Jim had called and had been trying to reach me.

Jim's sister had an apartment in my mom's friend's building. Jim was calling about my prom. Now that was an answered prayer. I wore all white and my navy guy wore the color navy. Jim and I use to go for walks on the beach in the summer. He shipped out for the Navy 3 years earlier. He asked me what year was my prom and I told him. I never thought that he would remember and leave that week open to come home and escort me on my prom. His sister was a very good seamstress and tailor made Jim's tuxedo. We went on my prom and my oldest brother was so proud that he gave us extra money for the photos. We had a great time. About 20 couples met in a hotel suite after the dinner. Our prom was at the Palmer House Hotel. We toasted champagne with the other couples. When Jim and I made it back to my house, the men in the parking lot began to tease Jim. They said that it was too early to bring a prom date home. It was 11:00 p.m. He ignored them and walked me to my door.

Since I didn't get to go to many house parties in our neighborhood; my cousin Deb would take me to parties with her. Mom helped raise her and she always had an invitation to somebody's party. These parties were always in very nice neighborhoods and we would always need a ride.

Deb seemed to want to fight if someone stood too close to me. If I would say anything to her about it, I would get cursed out too. She was in my wedding. She is still the same way. She is over-protective, yet full of love. We are like sisters. I talk to her about everything and we pray. I also brought a bible for her and a journal. I asked her to write in that journal all of the things that hurt. I asked her to mention disappointments and any un-forgiveness that she was pondering. I wanted her to forgive those who hurt her because she talked about things.

Journaling separates thoughts from us. Three days later, she called me on the telephone and asked me to sit down. I said, "Just tell me." She said, "No, sit down." I had just prayed for her at the hospital. She said that her doctors were crowded around her bed in disbelief. Her diagnosis had reversed.

She stated that the doctors were writing her medical summary in the hospital annals because of how a mass had formed inside protecting the rest of her body. I raised my voice, "Thank you Jesus!" Have you ever talked to someone every single day? If someone were to come and tell you something about that person; you would feel as though you already knew everything.

What if someone came and said, "Did you hear that so and so has cancer?" Your first reaction would be that you talk to that person everyday and that never came up. You would have your doubts about the news.

Well, a doctor diagnosed me with colon cancer. I told the doctor that I don't have that. She took me to a microscope and said that everywhere that you see shades of purple was cancer. I said, "No, it's not!" Then she talked to me about chemotherapy. Remember that prayer is talking to God. I said that I pray all of the time and I didn't hear anything about me being sick. The doctor went on to say that it was normal to deny this and that it would hit me eventually. She said that I needed to accept it. I told her it's not true. She wanted to see if it would spread so she scheduled my return date. I went on a FAST. I ate organic greens and drank lots of water. I prayed during the times that I normally would eat.

When I went back to the doctor they could not find anything wrong. The alleged cancer was gone. That same doctor who talked to me became confused. She was frowning after they retested me.

But she was smiling when she broke the news about the cancer. She said, "You have a lot of faith in your God." I said, "Yes, now you try Him for yourself."

Tragedies shape your life and your choices control your existence. I could have cried for weeks and then gone in for the chemotherapy. I could have called everybody I knew and told them that I was dying. I made a conscious choice to live.

I saw an interview about a cancer survivor who only watched comedy. He watched comedy all day and all night and laughed the cancer away. He is cancer free. He also kept negative talk completely away from him. He didn't use negative words and he didn't allow others to use them around him.

COURT REPORTING/COLLEGE

When I started college, I began as a stenographer. Court reporting wasn't something that I had planned. There was only 2 college's downtown that taught court reporting. McCormick College and Chicago College of Commerce both taught stenography. I attended Chicago College of Commerce and we were always competing with McCormick College. Court reporting is like learning another language by machine. It is a form of shorthand. I spent a lot of time studying and practicing on my machine. I made it to 220 w. p. m and usually the typing speed would be half of the shorthand. My typing speed was a little over 100 words per minute. I received an associate in stenography and an associate in legal secretarial. I decided that I truly didn't like court reporting. I did the internship at the courtrooms downtown, got my credits and finished. My mom said to at least finish. If any of us started something, mom made us finish.

COURT INTERNSHIP

NAME MARY SYKES   COURTROOM NO. 1306 p.m.

Thank you for participating as a court reporter in our Clinical Trial Advocacy mock jury trials. You have been assigned to the courtroom indicated above.

When your courtroom session breaks for lunch, please present the attached card at Burger King located directly across the street at 74 West Randolph. PLEASE NOTE: Eating, drinking and smoking are not permitted in the courtrooms.

Upon completion of the afternoon's trial proceedings, please report to the first floor Northwestern desk to pick up your $5.00.

I was riding on an El train early one Saturday morning about 7:30 a.m. and a man asked me was that a court reporting machine inside the case. I said, "Yes." He handed me his business card and said that when I graduate, I had a job waiting. The man was an older African American man who managed a court reporting firm. I used my machine shorthand while working but not in court.

MODELING

I used the machine to transcribe emergency calls made to dispatchers and I also used it for meeting minutes once I began my career. While in college, I was working full time during the day at McDonalds and later quit to finish court reporting school.

DePaul University was my next stop. I attended part time in the evenings while I worked as a full time stenographer in law enforcement administration. I went from a stenographer to an Administrator and loved my work. I enjoyed my classes and received my BA in communications. My major piece of work was a video and thesis on the history of modern dance. I created a modern dance research video and I actually performed in the video.

MARY MODELING

I was a modern dancer in high school who helped all the other dancers, so I decided to use those skills to do something that I like while gaining my degree. I also did a one woman drama show at DePaul. I did the very same show while in high school during the drama-fest. I received a standing ovation both times. I think the crowd liked it because it was comedy. They laughed hysterically. I love comedy.

I also modeled for a short time while in college. I modeled with my Italian friend named Thalia Valentin. She was blessed with beauty. At the time, she was a size 2. I was a size 3. I prayed for more pounds while in college because I was extremely thin.

Thalia would get me modeling jobs with her. We modeled at the "Marina 300 Club." Today it's still called "Marina City." Modeling is very hard work.

While in college I also made money selling cosmetic, perfume and I was the neighborhood beautician. I never went to school for cosmetology, but I would watch other people style hair. I learned from watching others.

School was always more important to me than a job. I was young and I knew I needed an education.

During my last semester at DePaul I did not tell my classmates or teachers that I was almost finished. I didn't want to draw attention and I also didn't want to be graded a certain way. Later, I found out that they list all graduates in the halls at the University. I don't know why I thought I could pull that off. I was sitting in class and the teacher announced all of the graduates that sat in that class and then looked at me. She said, "Why didn't you tell me that you were graduating?" There were about 3 graduates in this particular class. The graduates were asked to say something to the other students. I said that their hard work would pay off and that they can do it. I encouraged them. A few days later, I was asked by one of my teachers to report to the office.

I had heard of many horror stories about college students. I heard about teachers who didn't like certain students; and who had stopped them from graduating. I heard of many students repeating their last semester.

I didn't want to be that person. I went to the office. I sat at a table and waited for my teacher to join me. As I sat there I wondered just what did she want with me. Finally she came to the table and joined me. I smiled because I knew that she would always call me her favorite and we went on field trips together with the class. We always seemed to enjoy each other. I wanted to hug her but I smiled and said, "Hello." She said, "I hear that you are graduating?" I smiled and said "Yes." She said, "Just how do you plan on doing that if you are failing my class?" I did this humorous laugh because I thought she was joking. I said that I get A's and B's in your class. Her head was nodding a forward yes, but she said out of her mouth, "But it's my word against yours." She leaned forward close enough and said, "It's my word against yours."

She said that she feels that I am having problems in class now. Her body language said, "Yes, I know" while her words said, "No, I am not passing you."

She was smiling and my smile melted into a look of shock. I started to look around at all of the other teachers who were sitting at tables. I was wondering if any of them could hear what she was saying to me. I said, "But you always said that I was your favorite student?" She repeated, "That's your word against mine." She then wore this sick, crazy smile on her face.

I stood up and walked out of this meeting without looking back because the meeting was really a threat. I found a bathroom, went into the stall and fell to my knees and prayed. All of my hard work was being threatened. I called a co-worker of mine who was older and told her what was happening to me. She listened and said, "Yeah, my step daughter went through that same thing." I asked her what happened and she said that her daughter had to stay another semester. She also added that her daughter lived on campus out of state too. This only enhanced my feeling of betrayal. I went home and checked my answering machine. My guidance counselor was on my answering machine stating, "Mary, this is your guidance counselor. I have one of your teachers in my office and if what she's saying to me is true, you are not graduating." The words sent shock waves throughout my body. I didn't call him back that evening. I had worked so hard. My mentor was a doctor who had spent time with me assisting me in whatever I needed.

People had invested time and energy into my education. Prayer is definitely talking to God. I began talking to Him, saying how I felt and how I could not believe that someone could be so conniving. The person who I once thought was so kind soon became my enemy. Now as I am talking, I walked over to my closet. I still don't know how I ended up digging through a bin of papers. I kept a bin full of my college papers and assignments.

There were classes that I had taken but I later withdrew from them. If I got bored with a class, I would withdraw and do something else. One professor in particular was very nice. I always kept my professor's numbers. I kept their office and home numbers if they would give them to me. This particular professor worked for a law firm during the day and taught classes at night. He was an excellent teacher and I never had a problem with him. In fact, I had some wonderful teachers at DePaul. I called him and asked about the class that I withdrew. I asked him if there was a way that I could do an assignment to complete that credit and perhaps get the credit from him.

He said, "Sure Mary." I completed the assignment and faxed them to his office. He forwarded the credit to the school office.

That was all that I needed and my credits were complete. All of my grades were complete and I took a form called a "Grid" to the office. A grid is a sheet which summarizes every class and the credits. My counselor saw that I had all of the credits that I needed to graduate so he is the one who contacted the teacher who flipped on me.

I went to the university to pick up my cap and gown. I also received my tickets. I got on the elevator still shook-up, but yet excited too. I began to wonder what if I bumped into the teacher who tried to stop me from graduating.

I rehearsed in my mind about how that might have gotten under her skin to see me holding my cap and gown. When the elevator door opened, I was holding my cap and gown and sure enough, she was standing there waiting to step into the elevator. I was at the main level so I stepped off the elevator, walked around her and left. She seemed extremely upset. I was so grateful that God had allowed me the opportunity to graduate and get out of there that I stepped around her quietly and politely.

There was no need for any words or negative energy.

I read a scripture once that said, and I am paraphrasing it, "If you do the 'ah ha' thing after God has delivered you, He will turn that situation right back around on you." I was not about to do that at all.

I had been through too much. Pride was not standing in the way of my degree.

This was not the only obstacle during that time. I also ran out of money. I owed the university $800. I did not have $80; at least not for tuition. I had purchased my first piece of property at age 20 and my mortgage had to be paid. I was watching Dempsey J. Travis on television. He was talking about how he goes to basketball courts to look for young men who are wearing high school rings, but were not in college. He said that he helped them get into college. Mr. Travis was also one of the biggest property owners and real estate investors in Chicago.

I called his office and I was asked to come in and fill out a scholarship application. I walked into that interview on December 28, 1990. His office looked like the oval office at the White House. Twelve members of his scholarship committee sat around the big table. Mr. Travis sat at the end of the oval shaped table and I sat opposite of him. I handed each of them a copy of my resume and answered every question with confidence.

I needed the help and nothing was going to stop me. I had been through so much. At the end of the interview, Mr. Travis asked me had I read his book, "The autobiography of black Chicago." I had read it twice and I asked him to autograph my copy. I also got a copy for my mother.

When the interview was over Mr. Travis said to his committee, "Get this hard working young lady back in school." I could not walk into my last semester classes without paying that money. One of my final classes just happened to be using Mr. Travis' book, "The autobiography of black Chicago". I wrote him and told him that his book was being used and I sent him my syllabus where his book was listed. I had read in his book about how DePaul did not accept him. I said to him that he must be proud because now they are using his book to represent one of their classes. A couple of weeks later I received a letter of thanks and another check for $300 instructing me to pay for my books. I will never forget him for helping me. He died in 2009 and I attended his funeral. I shook hands with his widow and family and told them how much I appreciated and respected Mr. Travis. Many famous people attended this service out of respect for Mr. Travis. He could have helped anybody, but he chose to help me.

I also graduated from a school called, "Professional Business School". I studied computer science and I was class valedictorian. I enjoyed studying about computers and I met some wonderful people. At the end of my studies, I had funds remaining on my school account. I was expecting them to hand out refund checks before graduation.

The students that I talked to were not given any refunds. I researched and found out where the main campus was located. It was in St. Louis. I contacted them about my funds and by the time I arrived to school the next day, two men who were in charge of the school handed me a refund check. They asked me how I was able to discover that there was a main branch in St. Louis. I told them that I researched. There was never any talk about any other branches of this particular school. The dean of the school walked me into this meeting and stayed with me until they were finished talking to me. My graduation was that night. I was class valedictorian and they surprised me with a plaque during the ceremony. My lesson in this is "Stand up for what's right."

I received my masters in biblical studies while pregnant with my daughter Jessica. I am currently studying at Chicago Theological Seminary. I love learning. When I was younger, I studied all night. I noticed that educated people sat behind desks on the job. My mom actually had to tell me that I needed to go out with friends and have fun. During my first year in college she would always say, "All work and no play makes Mary a dull girl." I had a friend in court reporting school. We frequented the E2 night club because we got to see all of the famous comics and listen to live jazz. We would always talk about how hard it was to walk up and down the stairs. It was narrow. We often joked about how we'd be in trouble if there was ever a fire.

HONORABLE ELIJAH MUHAMMAD

When the E2 club had that stampede on February 17, 2003; my college friend called me on the telephone. I hadn't talked to her in a while. She said, "Did you hear about what happened?" I said, "Yes." She said, "Why did that happen to those people?" This made national headlines. There were 21 people killed and 50 hurt inside of the E2 club. My friend asked me why did God allow us to live but they didn't?" I simple told her, "Your parents were praying for you and my grandmother and parents were praying for me." Her dad was a pastor who had passed away. My grandmother was Ann Blackman and she was a praying woman. She was ordained and carried a ministry license the size of a driver's license in her wallet. She would go into the hospitals 24 hours a day and pray for the sick.

She had four sisters. Out of the five of them, only one of them is still alive. Her name is "Nancy." Now my great aunt Nancy is a retired widow and lives in Arkansas near her son. When she lived here in Chicago, she was the Honorable Elijah Muhammad's housekeeper. My grandmother use to pull up to the gated home and drop off her sister Nancy at work; and aunt Nancy would walk the rest of the way to the door. Aunt Nancy was the only one who entered Muhammad's home without using her pass. When I ask about how she liked working for him and his family she laughs. She said that it was great working for them.

They often joked about how he loved to snack at night. He would come to the kitchen late and tell auntie, "I'll bet you think we can really eat, huh?" My aunt says that's a beautiful family.

My grandmother could make the replica of the most expensive, Hollywood style coats and dresses. She was a professional seamstress. She even made me clothes. When I was in kindergarten she made my clothes for school with matching headbands to wear across my forehead. She also worked as a private caretaker. Once she arrived at work and was asked to, "Come down off the dressing." Some of the wives had a problem with her style. My grandma was the only black in the building at that time. She dressed neat and always wore comfortable dresses. She and my grandfather would dress up and meet other couples out for dinner and shows.

Her dining room table was full every Sunday and so was her house. My grandparents also traveled south to visit family in Arkansas, but mostly on holidays. They also caravanned by the car loads with aunts, uncles and cousins for weekend outings.

When my grandmother was a very young mother, she had a neighbor who gave her problems. The family was "The Browns" and they lived in the same building. This was before my grandmother moved into a house. They really gave my grandmother a hard time.

While my grandfather was at work one particular day, my grandmother decided to pick up her children from school rather than have them walk home. When she arrived home with her children, the Brown family came outside. There were 5 women and 2 men who confronted my grandmother. My grandfather had left a jackhammer in the car. My grandmother grabbed it and began to swing and yell, "Children get in the house and don't come out!" "Get in the house and don't come out!" She swung and swung that jackhammer until it landed to the foreheads of all 7 of them.

The police were called to the scene. When they arrived, all of the Browns had a cut on their foreheads in the same exact spot. My grandmother said that the police could not believe that she had acted alone. This incident appeared in the local newspaper. This is just one of the many stories that I was told by relatives.

My grandfather invented a lifter that carries package. The only proof that we have is the newspaper article with a photo of him holding his bonus check for $25. It was later on in life that my grandmother accepted her calling and began training for ministry. My grand dad had passed on. Nobody that I know prays like my grandmother. She had a kneeling altar that I kept and I use it today.

She did not lock her doors because she said that the angels were watching over her home. She never had a break-in either. I would spend the weekends with her. A couple of times I walked in her house and there would be about 10 people from Africa wrapped in Kente cloth sleeping everywhere. She would motion for me to keep quiet and do not wake them. I would whisper, "Who are they?" She would say, "They're your cousins."

If she saw a woman with children on any bus stops she would stop and drive them home. It never failed and I would be scared out of my mind. I don't ever remember any person turning her rides down. Once it was raining and there was a woman with 4 children waiting for the bus. I thought to myself, "Lord, do not allow them to accept the ride." I didn't know them. But they got into her car and she drove them home. I was young and didn't understand her type of ministry work. Those who operate the way my grandmother lived are called "Anomaly." They are different and separated from common rules. They don't fit in because their thinking is not negotiable. They trust God with their whole hearts. When she prayed things happened. She would tell me what was going on around me and what I was thinking. She loved all people and color didn't matter. People mistook her for her race and really didn't know what color she was at times.

They would call her "Mixed." Her eyes would look gray and sometimes blue. She once took care of 3 Jewish boys. Their dad was a doctor and the mother was a Jewish school teacher. When the parents died, my grandmother petitioned to raise the boys as her own. During this particular time it was said that the boys would be better off with their Jewish grandmother in New York. One of the boys ran away to be with my grandmother. Of course she had to return him.

Before my grandmother passed away, 2 of the boys she helped raise visited her often. I can remember one particular occasion when my grandmother was hospitalized. One of the boys became an attorney. He paid her hospital physician to make a home visit. Everything that she needed was given to her. She was already doing fine for herself, but they made things even better for her. During her final days my mom moved my grandmother into her spare bedroom in her home.

Mom moved her across the hall from her bedroom in order to take proper care of her. Whatever my grandmother needed she got it. The family rotated and volunteered. On my grandmother's last trip to the hospital, I went to visit her at 5:00 a.m. Many hospitals allow more time for visits when they know the patient's health is declining.

JESUS IS THE ANSWER

I asked the minister who officiated our wedding to please come to the hospital to pray since our pastor was unable to go. My father-in-law accompanied him and they prayed. I never forgot their kindness on that day. I would go to the hospital and read her favorite scriptures. The last scripture that I read was Psalm 91. When I got to the exit door of her hospital room I stopped and turned around and looked at her. I somehow knew that it was the last time that I would see her alive. She knew too because she said, "It's okay because I know where I am going." Everybody called my grandmother "Peggy." She once told me that when I skipped a day reading her scriptures it felt like a whole week.

We all need someone in life who can pray with us. We wake up to some unexpected news sometimes. There are many disasters, floods, tsunamis, tornados, and fires. People are selfish. People are in pain. Some houses are not homes and people don't know what is going to happen. The schools do not have all of the answers. The welfare and the government don't have all of the answers. Jesus is the answer. Racism is simply people passing down bad behavior and training the next generation to hate. People learn to hate. Love is innate. They are trained to think differently about someone of another race. As a young girl, I can remember some uncomfortable fieldtrips. I remember blacks being deprived of using certain washrooms.

I can also remember going to get financial help for school at a community center in an African American neighborhood and a woman asked me, "What color are you?" She didn't want to serve me. When I arrived back to work, I told my co-workers what had happened to me and they were like, "Yeah, Mary you look a little mixed." My own race tried to reject me. I was in a drug store once and an African American woman and a Korean woman were arguing. Words had exchanged and the Korean woman said, "Oh, why don't you go back to the ghetto?" The African American woman said, "Oh, no, why don't you go back to Korea where they are killing your mother f---ing -----. I spell curse words even when I am trying to tell my husband about something that someone said. But my husband always says, "Mary, just say it." I tell him that I can't say that word. He said you are spelling it so just say it. In other words, you are still promoting the word. He feels that it's not worth repeating. I think I like getting my point across so I still spell certain words.

I was at college once in line paying for a book and 2 Caucasian young ladies were talking. One said, "I got the job, a new apartment, I have a great life and I'm white." She was saying that life was better for her because she was white. Many people can say, "Well, many blacks do well for themselves also. Who can challenge the fact that racism does exist?

I was in line at the bank and 2 Caucasian young men were talking. One said to the other, "I love life. If I were black and stole a candy bar I may get time in jail. But since I'm white I can say I killed somebody and I'd get a slap on the wrist and they'll tell me, 'Well just don't do it again okay'." Then they both laughed. There are people who could care less about color. They look at people's souls. Racism is a sickness. I had an Irish boss who wanted me to marry her son. She asked me was the age difference a problem. Her son was about 3 years younger. He ended up marrying an Irish woman, and I married a black man.

One of my classmates at Chicago Theological Seminary is Margaret Tate. She told me that she remembers when the high schools in Arkansas were preparing to integrate in 1954. According to her, she lived in Pine Bluff, Arkansas at the time. She was in elementary school. It was not clear which high school she would enroll because of the new plan for integration. Ms. Tate remembers everyone waiting. They waited to see what would happen in Little Rock, Arkansas regarding integrating.

She remembers that after Little Rock high school was integrated in 1957, it paved the way for Central High School in Little Rock to integrate and then Dolloway High School; which is where Ms. Tate integrated. In Little Rock, Arkansas, this opened the door for Ms. Tate's community to enlarge because minority students were bused from Pine Bluff, Arkansas into the white neighborhoods.

This gave the minority students better opportunities for education.

According to Ms. Tate, she remembers the National Guard standing in the halls outside of the classrooms where black students had recently integrated. She also remembers how blacks were not allowed to speak up for themselves and she remembers signs on washroom doors separating races. Today, some people find ways to segregate in their own way.

When I was in court reporting school we were very close to the teachers.

Two ladies by the names of Mae S. Glassbrenner and Lucille Horstmirer started this school in a little shack in 1950. When I initially entered the school you could count the blacks on one hand. By the time I finished there were many. The instructors did not care what color you were, they were about perfection and sending out the best court reporters.

One instructor in particular stated that we were all friends. Then he went on to say that a lot of blacks say "Axed" instead of "Asked.". The teachers didn't care. Correction was necessary and that is what they believed. They also complimented us on our professionalism and everybody carried a dictionary with them. One day our Dean, Ms. Horstmirer called me into her office. She said, "I've been noticing your work." She handed me 4 books from her personal library and asked me to polish my proofreading skills. I was getting A's and B's.

Eventually I was getting papers back and I would hardly ever get corrections for spelling errors.

Most of the students at Chicago College of Commerce worked at law firms.

No matter what your color, we were all very well educated. Everyone spoke with proper English or you were corrected. I got many scholarships. I studied all night long. Mom said that I needed to be the smartest in class in order to be considered equal.

There was a game we use to play in class called, "Sudden death." This meant that you took dictation on the court reporting machine. Sometimes the speed was 220 w.p.m.

I typed fast because I stayed up all night practicing. I studied all night long about 3 nights a week. The game was that you raised your hand to read back the dictation and if you missed a word, you stopped and the next person would pick up where you left off. Well, I would read so long that they would clap. I had a couple of instructors that got tired of me reading the dictation. If I had every word then I should be able to read every word. The better I was at transcribing, the better my chances were for success. Other students could do it. A teacher finally began to stop me and say you missed a word. But some other student would intervene and say, "No, she didn't."

I would go to Mr. O's class and he was like a dad to a lot of the Caucasian students. When I would read my dictation for a long period of time in his class, he would stop me, look out into his classroom and yell, "You sorry bunch of ...." "You are going to sit there and let her out-do you?" "You poor excuse for ...." He cursed them out a couple of times. My friend Dee who sat next to me said that I should stop raising my hand. She would say, "Let them have it." I kept reading if I had it. Part of our grade came from class participation. Mr. O graded me well, "A's".

He called on me when he wanted to and other times he would not call on me. I didn't try for the license because after completing my internship at the courtrooms here in Chicago, I decided I didn't like court reporting. Of course my mom made me finish.

Graduating was simply someone from the office tapping my classmate on the shoulder and saying, "Hey, pass this degree over to Mary." There weren't any graduation ceremonies. Everyone in class typed over 100 w.p.m. and shorthand was always close to 200 w.p.m. or above. Every student was also a Notary Public because court reporters had to be notaries. The instructors got the very best out of all of us.

The teachers were nice but there was one other teacher whom I remember that was very old. She had these books that were so old that the pages were deteriorating. The books contained courtroom cases from the early 1900s or earlier. Whenever this teacher would ask a student to read the material, that student would always stop. They called African American people animal names in court back then. They were treated as non-humans. Once the passage was read, the teacher would laugh and say "Oops." Then she would sit the book on her desk. I can remember staring at that book and wanting to burn it. That teacher was eventually fired.

There is no excuse for this type of behavior but some people are stuck in their ways. Others choose not to change. It's about choices. Our choices are the outline for our future. We must never allow racism to be our excuse for not accomplishing something. If no one encourages you, encourage yourself.

I took my mom and other family members on a carriage ride in Chicago's Gold Coast. It is a beautiful area downtown. I love looking at the houses. We had a tour and enjoyed the brisk air as the horseshoes clicked along the streets. After the ride, I decided to take them for lunch.

I asked them all to wait while I walk across Michigan Avenue to get the car out of the lot.

I went up the elevator and used my card to pay for the parking but the machine would not take the card. I didn't understand it because my card was fine and I used it often. There was a Caucasian man standing there and he said, "Oh, that machine always does that. You can go someplace else and your card will work." He then said, "Here, let me." He pulled out a black credit card, stuck it into the machine and a paid receipt printed out. The cost was $26.00. He smiled and said, "There." I was so surprised. My mouth was opened, eyes wide and I turned and looked at him and I said, "But your credit card was charged and." He looked very close to my eyes and said, "There, that's the expression I wanted. Now enjoy the rest of your day." Then he quickly walked away. I was standing there holding a paid in full receipt.

Here was a perfect stranger paying for my parking. He was older and simply wanted to do something generous for someone. I was so grateful and I did yell as he left, "Hey, thanks!"

Mr. Silas Parnell was a great pioneer. He was African American. He helped so many people get into school. He helped students find scholarships too. It didn't matter about race. If you were black, white, Asian, Puerto Rican, Japanese, Chinese, whatever, he helped.

I remember traveling to a project building inside of low income housing to get a scholarship for school. I remember different races going to the same location to get help from Mr. Parnell. He passed away but I will never forget him because he was fair and he believed in education.

If this were a perfect world, everyone would wake up, forget the past and forgive every wrong done. The color of a person's skin tone wouldn't make a difference. Your gender wouldn't make a difference. Your style won't make a difference. Everyone could live in whatever neighborhood they choose.

The school and job you wanted would be completely a matter of intelligence. There are churches that do not want mixed races in their congregation.

A church should be like a hospital where sick people go to get better. Some hospitals discriminate.

We have got to allow our children to know that they can do anything. Other's opinions do not have to be our reality.

My youngest daughter writes in journals a lot. She loves writing. At the age of 9 she decided to write a book. By age 12 she became a published author who had a successful book signing at the local library. She also wrote for her school newsletter. We are proud of her because in spite of all that she does; she is humble.

If we allowed it, Jessica would stay up all night studying. She wants to get into the best college. Jessica is not perfect and she does make mistakes as we all do. When she does something great we let her know how proud we are as parents. She wants to pattern her life after her parents. My husband and I graduated from universities.

Do whatever it is that you choose to do. Do not fear. FEAR is False Evidence Appearing Real. Go for it! Jessica is being raised in the church. We make sure that she attends bible class and youth worship. The BIBLE is Basic Instructions Before Leaving Earth. The Word of God helps to keep all of us in order. It keeps us focused in the right direction.

Do what's best for you. Don't do what's best for other people. Let them live their lives and you live yours.

Maya Angelou was my mentor. I listened to her and when she was in town I made it a point to go and hear her speak. She recently passed away.

She once said that "If you tell someone "No" and they don't hear it, they are trying to control you." Use your time wisely because there is no layaway for time. All you've got is right now. My little brother often says that "No" is a complete sentence. I am so proud of my brother John. He is a psychotherapist with his own practice in Chicago's Hyde Park area. There is a waiting list for his services. He also teaches at the University of Chicago. He wanted his own practice and nothing stopped him.

My oldest brother Mark is good with fixing cars and he now has his own auto mechanic shop.

My brother Brian has had many challenges in life but never allow them to stop him. He finally figured out what he wants to do. He is the second to the oldest. He has a big heart and everyone who meets him knows it. I say that because he once took his coat off in freezing temperatures to hand it to a stranger who didn't have a coat. When the family questioned him once he arrived home, his answer was that he had another one. He also saved 2 lives on the streets after witnessing some near death experiences. He has paramedic experience.

He now works in hospital nutrition. One of the best things about his ministry is that he tells great jokes while he serves others. Ministry should be inside of your heart. It should be included in everything that you do. You should live it every day. It should show in your conversations and your actions.

Many people go to church and then go home and tell everybody, "Hey, I went to church." Sometimes it's a ritual. You can drive to the building, shake hands, sing, pray and listen to the sermon. If you leave and go right back to doing things that are unpleasing to God, then that visit is meaningless.

Once the Spirit gets on the inside of you, you won't be the same.

There is a love and kindness that grows on the inside. That Spirit will put you in check the next time you want to do something that will eventually hurt somebody else. That Spirit makes you love people and that includes everybody.

I had to get saved for real. I didn't mind fighting when someone tried to mess with me. I didn't mind cursing you out either. My heart had to be changed in order for me to grow spiritually. I went from quiet to cursing.

Saved people are in this world but not of this world. That is why saved people have "Home-going services" when they pass away.

They don't call it funeral services. The service is a celebration for saved people because the end of this world is not eternal death for us. It is eternal life because we transition into Heaven. We are children of light and not darkness.

Unsaved sinners are repeat offenders who love evil. They plot and plan and scheme evil deeds. They live in darkness because their deeds are evil. When you are saved for real, you are children of light. You are not trying to hide anything. You love people for real. You want to get along with everyone for real.

I was watching the news and 3 people jumped into the Chicago River around midnight and it was almost below zero outside.

The 1ˢᵗ guy went in after his cell phone had landed on some ice. When the ice broke he went under so his 2 friends dived in trying to rescue him. The 1ˢᵗ two medical students died and the 3ʳᵈ friend who jumped in survived. Many people would judge and say why try to save a cell phone? Many people do things and we never know why we do them. I don't think that young man traded his life for a cell phone. He made a quick decision and as a result of his decision he died. I was at home and my husband was on his way home from work. I heard a woman crying outside. I went to my front door and there was a woman lying on the sidewalk in front of my house and I saw blood. I went outside and asked her what happened.

She said that she only wanted her grandmother. I asked her again, "Who cut you?" She said that her husband had thrown her through a glass door. Both of her wrist and arms were bleeding terribly. I ran inside my home and grabbed my cell phone and 2 drying towels. I tied both towels around her arms and they were soaked. I took my cell phone and called for an ambulance. As I waited, the dispatcher was asking me to find out her name and where she lived. By this time other neighbors were coming outside. All of a sudden a guy who looked to be in his 20s ran up to me and said, "Let her die she didn't raise me." A woman walked over stating that he was the hurt woman's son. It seemed to be a spirit of drug abuse on this young man.

The lady also stated that he helped do that to her and that the injured woman had just lost her mother. That explained why she was crying for her grandmother. Then I began to recognize this woman. I remember them moving in their house. I do remember thinking, "She is so pretty that she would make Halle Berry nervous."

Then 2 young children about the ages of 6 and 8 came over crying. They were her youngest children. I asked the 8 year old to hold his sister's hand and I told him that it was very important that he not let go of his sister's hand.

I then told the 6 year old little girl that her mom was going to be okay. The girl was shaking the way a person does who is having a seizure. Then I noticed she began to calm down. She was worried about her mom.

The oldest son began threatening me about helping. Here is the perfect example of how you will never know if you'd die for a stranger. I was holding this lady's cuts to stop her from losing so much blood because she passed out. Blood was all over me and I looked at her oldest son and said, "Whatever you are going to do, do it because I am not letting her go."

I began to pray. All of a sudden my husband came home and the ambulance also pulled up with a squad car. The lady woke up and asked me to call her grandmother. She began to call out her grandmother's telephone number. I dialed the number and allowed her to speak to her grandmother. That woman lived. I do not know if she is still with her husband or not because they moved. I can see myself telling someone else that they should have mind their own business. When this happened to me, I jumped right in and helped a dying woman. The Word of God says, "Honor your father and mother". It doesn't say unless they didn't raise you. That older son who wanted her to die was completely out of control. Some people help others and some choose not to help anyone. I've been praying my whole life. Even when I was young, using bad language and fighting; I was a desperate soul and did only what I knew how to do.

The older I get the more I pray. Prayer comes with the package once you are married.

I have a blended family. I gained my 2 oldest children at the altar on my wedding day.

After 5 years into our marriage we finally had my daughter Jessica. Currently we have been together 21 years and marriage for 18 of those years. We must be so careful with how we raise our children in the world that we live in today.

My husband takes Jessica on outings, and my brothers also take her on outings. They open doors for her and show her the way a young lady should be treated. When she starts dating, she will know what to expect.

I am raising Jessica to be the best person that she can possibly become.

She is learning about the great depression at school. When I am driving her to school, I take a certain route on the way. There is a line of people outside of a community center. That line goes around the corner every day. They wait outside to get free food whether it is raining or freezing cold.

Jessica told me that the line was similar to the one she saw in a photo about the great depression. I explained to her that they are lined up for the same things that she is reading about in those books. So many people are laid off and jobless right now.

So many people have no healthcare. President Barack Obama passed a law just recently that allows every citizen a right to healthcare. Families are struggling and many are getting link cards in order to receive food.

Almost half of Chicago's black families were on some form of public welfare in the early 1900s. I sometimes wonder whether that's still the case. When I was growing up we called our homeless "Hobos." They wore ripped up dirty clothes and hid in tunnels, woods and train freight cars.

During the great depression, every day someone was evicted on the blocks for non-payment of rent. We see this today where they sit furniture outside on the sidewalks because someone could not pay their rent or mortgage.

During the early 1930s the neighbors would come over and help the owner of the furniture sit on top of the furniture so that the sheriff could not remove the furniture. Fast forward to today and you will see how the neighbors will peep out of their windows and point, but they won't dare help someone sit on some furniture.

Many of us have relatives who fought in the wars or worked the street cars. Some older relatives worked in the steel mill, coal miners or were maids cleaning houses and caring for other people's children. Our forefathers sold papers, lemonade, shined shoes, and carried bags in order to contribute to their households. Many were clerks, Pullman porters, barbers, beauticians and tailors. Some worked the stockyards and factories making whatever money they possibly could make because the recession reached everybody.

In 1950 there was also a recession and many men could not find work. The women took jobs as maids. Does any of this sound familiar? There are so many people today, in the year 2015 getting the "Helping care" jobs as in-home care-takers. These workers are hard working people. The only difference is that all races have a chance to get this service and if you cannot afford to pay for it, the government pays for the seniors who are sick and need assistance.

Having the right to vote is so powerful. Many people do not realize just how powerful it is to vote. Many elected officials are making it impossible for some to live comfortably. This has been going on for a long time.

Southern states actively adopted poll taxes in the early 1900s as a way to deprive the rights of minority voters.

The black vote reconstructed government. Blacks walked miles to pay that poll tax. They marched for equal rights to vote and some were murdered for organizing voter's registration drives. Many Caucasians died also for fighting for equal rights of all people.

We all know someone who sits at home and do not press their way out to vote. All U. S. citizens have the right to vote except felons or the mentally disabled. States charge a type of fee to get a state ID or driver's license. When you need one of these in order to vote; can it be argued that the fee is a poll tax? In each case, everyone has to pay. If you have the right to vote, do it. Your vote does count.

All people should be treated the same, but everyone is not going to do it. That is why it is so important to remember who you are in life. Some people were raised to believe that they do not have to respect others.

As long as there is racism, our country will remain sick. We must care about one another. If you ever discovered where the "Yo mama" jokes came from, you'd never tell another one.

MAYOR HAROLD WASHINGTON

Those jokes originated from the slave masters. They talked about the slaves and their families as they worked in the fields. There are illiterate people in all races. Some just put who they choose in certain positions.

Buying and selling dope contributes to killing off generations of people. Too many of our young men are incarcerated and walking around inside of jails wearing uniforms with sagging pants because belts are not allowed. Sagging is also a sign of sexual availability in prisons. They come out of jail and continue to wear the pants sagging. This is because that is what they are use to and now the young people have created a type of style. Many know that's where the style came from and others don't. Some are just following and not creating.

As I come to a close in my current career, I can't help but thank God for all that I have endured. I met some wonderful people. I learned so much in 30 years. Many of us do it and some work even longer. I held four positions and each were promotions. One position was a lateral move that turned into a promotion. My very first professional position was called "Stenographer." Harold Washington was a lawyer and the 1st black Mayor of the City of Chicago. He had so much to do with me getting my job in law enforcement. I keep a book to read with me at all times because of him. There is no perfect job. There are no perfect people.

Make the best out of your career. If you are working and find it difficult to get along with certain people; pray and love people. "Perfect love cast out fear." If you love people sincerely and you fervently pray for people; disappointments won't hurt and you won't fear. People are not perfect and we aren't either. Some prefer to switch careers. It's totally up to you.

I got on an elevator one day with a man whose son was murdered. He turned and looked at me and said, "Laugh as much as you can." Tomorrow is not promised to any of us. On April 13, 2011, I decided to take lunch around 12:00 noon. I wanted a small 7-layer salad. I decided to take the bus to get the salad since it was several blocks away. When I boarded the bus; something came over me and said, "Something is going to happen." I looked out of the window as I was thinking, "Lord, should I get off this bus?" Immediately as I questioned what to do, a man hit the left side of the bus; which was pointed northbound. He was trying to turn right in front of the bus. My right arm hit a pole that separated the seats and my hip slammed into the lady next to me. People were falling into each other and a crippled man slid to the floor. The driver sharply turned the wheel to the right and jumped the curb. When we came to a halt, the driver yelled, "Is everyone okay?" As we were fumbling around this bus, I was not afraid and I felt warned.

Somehow I knew that I would be okay. I remember thinking, "I guess a 7-layer salad is out of the question." I called my husband and he showed up on the scene in about 15 minutes. I then called my job. I explained what had just happened and my co-worker yelled, "Oh, my God Mary, are you alright?"

I said, "Yes." They said for me not to worry and they would take good care of me. All of a sudden squad cars showed up in addition to the one already on the scene. I was taken care of very well. It was not the bus driver's fault at all and I made sure that the authorities knew. My neck was sore and I didn't feel a thing in my back until the next day. I took a little time off work because of this incident. If you are ever in an accident and you feel fine, wait a while before making a final decision about your health. You may be hurt but do not realize it until later.

When my dad passed away, this was a very hard time for me. I had to travel far because dad moved out of state. I don't know what I would have done if my little brother John Jr. and my husband were not assisting me. My father-in-law and family were praying. My co-workers were also very generous during this very difficult time in my life.

I have good memories of my career and some not so good memories. A lady said to me once, "How can you work for that supervisor of yours? There is no way that I could do that.

You are strong." She had quit and told me that everybody is not as strong as me. I knew what was happening to me. I made a decision to do my job and I worked hard. If something was due by Friday, I would have it finished before the due date. There are too many complains on layaway.

A preacher once said that life is 10% (what happened to you); and 90% (how you responded).

I try to always speak kindly to everyone. "A sharp tongue can cut your own throat." My co-workers celebrate my birthdays and when I was pregnant I was given the best baby shower. They gave me my first shower and my family gave me an additional baby shower. I have delivered weapons but never had to shoot one. I learned how to decide whether a particular gun was used in a homicide. I have also driven a detective car to escort new recruits. My office had the best view of the City of Chicago.

Jessica's school was directly across the street from my office. This was very convenient for us.

Try to find something good to smile about. Life has enough disappointment. Find the good part and meditate on the good more than the bad. Use your 90% in a positive way. Other people will complain about your environment more than you.

If you are enduring a challenging season in life; do not forget to pray. Things are not going to be great all of the time. Sometimes when people do not know everything about you, they will make something up. They create stories when they are afraid to ask questions.

There was a man who worked for a well-known company. He had a position that caused him to make major decisions. He was well-liked by his co-workers and made a very handsome salary.

He was Caucasian and worked very hard. He put his all into this work. He didn't miss any days and was never late. One day he had a heart attack at work and died. He fell to the floor and was gone.

As popular as he was on this job, a boss rushed to have an employee quickly punch him out and take him off the clock. One of his co-workers told me about what happened. This story takes me back to something that my mom has always told me. "Do a good job and remember that you are a machine to them." My mom told us that we are there to do a job and nothing else. She would always tell us, "You can be replaced."

Take a good look at your life right now. It is not what you went through, but it is really about who you have become since you went through it.

We all have an inside voice. Sometimes that voice warns you to do certain things and other times it warns you not to do things.

Once, I was talking to my husband on my office telephone. We were both at work but took breaks. We talked a few minutes and then I said, "Let me get back to work." He agreed and we both hung up. I began to type and that strong inside voice began to urge me to go home. I looked at the clock and it was 2:00 p.m. I had already taken lunch.

I then went to my supervisor and asked to be excused. I didn't know why but I had a feeling that I needed to leave and go home. The feeling was strongly intense.

I could not ignore this feeling so I went straight home. I parked my car in front of the house. I usually park in the garage. I saw neighbors standing on the sidewalks. When I got out of my car my next door neighbor rushed over to my car saying, "I am so sorry, so sorry." She took for granted that I knew what had happened. I didn't know what she was talking about. All I knew to do was to go home.

No one called me and I didn't have a cell phone at this particular time. My neighbor took me inside of her house and it was burned. It was unlivable. I was stunned. I said, "Why are you apologizing to me?" She then went on to say that the flames had attached to my home. I ran out of her house and over to mine.

The neighbors began to say how another neighbor attached water hoses together and held them to my kitchen window to stop the flames from burning my house.

I ran in and my kitchen blinds were melted. The kitchen window was cracked from top to bottom. It looked as if the slightest tap would cause it to burst. I could smell smoke in my home but no other damages.

My next door neighbor looked around and began to cry again. I told her not to worry and that everything was okay. She was offering to pay for damages. I said, "No." I was sure my husband would feel the same way about waiving any fees for damages. She began to cry again. I walked her home and called my husband and asked him to come home.

He asked me how I knew to leave work and go home. He had remembered that I told him that I was getting back to work. My answer to him was that I had a strong feeling about coming home so I did. After that, my husband became our block club president. This happened in 1998. We started a block club telephone tree and he selected me as his secretary.

We all have an inward witness. That is the witness that is inside of your spirit telling you to go. When we learn how to completely follow our inward witness, things will change.

We all have this but we must activate it on the inside. That is why it is so important to pray. God will guide you into every affair of life.

Remember that God will never lead you to do something harmful to anyone. The Spirit blesses people. The Spirit gives people a chance and forgives. It doesn't insult people and deliberately cause people to hurt.

One thing that you can give away and still keep is your words. Troubles do not last always. Try your best to be "On fire" about your passion in life. If you mess up, that's only an opportunity for you to begin again. If someone is trying to put down your accomplishments; that has nothing to do with what you are doing. Their motive is their problem and not yours.

Find time for yourself. Do things that enrich your life. Relax and find time to meditate. Go for a walk on your lunch hour.

I have seen celebrities on a regular basis while working. I took a walk on State Street during my lunch hour and I saw Oprah. She was wearing a green dress. I often wonder if that was the very last time she ever walked alone without security. This was in the 1980s. She was wearing sunglasses. My mouth flew open and I was extremely surprised. She put her hands together in the prayer position and motioned "Please." She didn't want to draw attention to herself. She shook my hand and motioned for me to keep walking.

I gave her respect and kept it moving.

One of my favorite movies is "A Bronx Tale."

This movie was directed by the actor Robert De Niro. He also starred in this film. My husband and I were vacationing in Hawaii and on the 8th day we got tired of all of the Hawaiian luou parties and tours. We took our rental car and went across the freeway to rent a movie. We rented "A Bronx Tale." It is an excellent movie. Well, something funny happened.

I was at work one day and I was leaving my office to take a break.

I looked at a man who was signing the log book. He turned and smiled at me. I said, "Hello." By the time I got to the next room I stopped. I thought to myself, "That was Mr. Robert De Niro!" When I went back into the office, he turned and began to laugh. He probably laughed because of the silly expression on my face. I did a shy hello again and very quietly kept it moving. The first time that I looked into his face he just seemed like someone familiar; perhaps because I watch his movies so much. Mr. Michael Jordan is another talented person that would frequent our office. He was always nice and polite.

Celebrities are human and God is no respecter of persons. When we meet someone familiar or famous, we really should give them the same energy that we give any other person.

MEET THE PRESIDENT

We are all special. My husband and I were meeting with Pastor Ambercrombie. At the time, we would attend his marriage ministry weekend events. He also provided us with wise counsel. He was running late for our meeting with him, so we waited. Finally, he walked in with then, Senator Barack Obama. My husband was familiar with Obama. We all shook hands and as the pastor was preparing to meet with us, we got a chance to talk with Barack Obama. He was impressed about us as a couple. He complimented us for being in church.

We had a nice chat and then we moved right into our meeting with the pastor.

Pastor Ambercrombie said, "Keep your eyes on him, you are going to see more of him." Soon after, we watched Obama announce his candidacy for President of the United States and he won.

I mentioned how things were in my old neighborhood. Barack Obama worked as a community organizer in Altgeld. He worked tirelessly in a fight regarding better living conditions for the residents.

We should all do what we can to help others. After my retirement, I plan to volunteer more at Jessica's school. She will have her mom at home during her high school years.

I can remember going to her elementary school with other parents to wash desk, chairs and bulletin boards so that the school wouldn't have to pay for extra janitorial services.

We all made donations. The parents that showed up to scrub the school furniture also demonstrated to our children how much we cared.

Currently, I sit on the expulsion board at Jessica's school. We decide whether a child should stay in the school or get expelled. The committee is made up of the school staff, management and a parent. We meet after fights, verbal altercations, et cetera.

I noticed how social media has a big impact on how the fights get started. Our youth have so many ways to communicate with each other. They forget the real purpose for why they use certain devices. Social media is not meant for gossip. I want to encourage all of the youth.

If you are using social media and someone is insulting you and belittling you, separate yourself from the drama. If the conversation is not adding to your life in a positive way, get away from it.

This is why it is so important to be involved in a good ministry. I apply the Word to life experiences. People want to know how to handle the disappointing child, mate, co-worker, loved one, associate or friend. Some people wonder how marriage last for long periods of time.

I can teach my students how to quote every scripture that relates to their problem. But if I can show them how to keep enough love inside of their hearts; that's healing for their souls.

Forgiveness is not for the other person. I have said this before. Forgiveness is for you! Sometimes what we say doesn't teach as much as how we walk as a person.

A woman told me that she was planning on going to church to get saved. She said that she had to get herself together first. Many people think that way. That is really the opposite of reality.

We are supposed to get saved so that we can get it right.

Saved people aren't completely fixed; we are on a spiritual journey. The church is designed to be your rehabilitation. We'll never be perfect! We are a daily work in progress. We have to set goals for ourselves and move that goal to line up to where we are now. If there are any stumbling blocks in your way get rid of them. The way we live our lives teaches those who are watching.

I teach that we all must develop a relationship with God through conversations the same way that we develop friendships in the natural. Prayer is talking to God and meditation is listening to God. Take a walk and meditate. I never thought I'd be a jogger but I am now. Relax yourself and find time for yourself.

I enjoy working with youth because when they begin to think, sparks fly. We plan activities to utilize the youth's talents. There is singing, praise dancing, poetry, preaching and testimonials. Every time we meet is one step closer to keeping our youth off the streets of Chicago.

There is too much shooting and violence going on around our streets, basketball courts, parks and playgrounds. Our youth know that they have options. Life is a teacher. This is earth school 101.

The bible is about love and life. I teach that the best way to get rid of your enemy is to increase their capacity for happiness and well being. I teach my students that they have to be the change that they want to see in the world.

You can try to help people and sometimes it will be clear that some people do not want your help. Sometimes you can do the right thing for the wrong person. Once you realize this, it should be clear not to help the one that doesn't really want your help.

Have you ever stopped and wondered why you worship the religion that you do? Many are born into certain religions. Many grow up and decide to switch religions.

I am Christian because I believe in Jesus and so does my family. My dad's name was "John." He was born catholic because he was raised by his catholic grandparents.

He later converted to Baptist and joined the Baptist Church. He met my mom in the choir stand at church. Our family has worshipped in the same church in Chicago since the 1950s. Our maternal family tree dates back to the 1800s and everyone there are Christians. Some people attend churches because of location or convenience. Some join churches because the church provides transportation.

In 1850, my maternal ancestors moved from South Carolina to Arkansas and my great-great grandfather, Pastor Louis Keith, established First Baptist Church in Eudora, Arkansas in 1857. Today, this is the oldest church in Eudora. Many generations of our family worship in this church even today. My maternal grandparents were a part of the great migration and moved from Arkansas to Chicago on their wedding day.

My grandfather's name was "Willie". He was in World War II. My grandmother, Annie named my mother after her dad because she didn't think that my grandfather would come home from fighting in the war.

She named her first born and my mother, "Willie Mae."

In 1865, General Robert E. Lee surrendered to General Ulysses S. Grant to end the Civil War. My paternal great grandparents were a part of the great migration.

SYKESVILLE, ARKANSAS

My paternal great grandfather's name was Ulysses Grant Sykes. He married my great grandmother, "Betty." They moved from Sykesville, Arkansas to Chicago in the 1940s. The town Sykesville was full of residents with the name "Sykes." I remember my great grandfather wearing a beat up old green army cap in the 1970s. I would ask him why he wouldn't take off that old hat. He would say, "I was in World War I!"

That old hat was the hat he wore in the war and it gave him pride. Growing up we weren't too involved in church. Everybody went occasionally. I never participated in anything in a church until I got married. My husband, Titus talked to me about becoming a part of the body of Christ before we even got married.

I followed my husband to church in Melrose Park for ten years after we got married. We currently worship closer to home. Titus plays the saxophone. He was a part of the music ministry most of his life. Today my youngest daughter and I follow my husband to various churches. He plays his horn for Pastor's on call.

Jessica's instrument of choice is the piano. Titus accepted Christ at the age of 3 years old. My daughter Jessica was the same age when she accepted Christ and my father-in-law, assisted in baptizing them both.

A PRISON EXPERIENCE

Pastor McNelty was a great pastor. Once I married my husband, Pastor and his wife treated me as their child because of my husband.

Pastor McNelty started the "H. McNelty high school." Before he died he told me that he was proud of me. When we worshipped there, He also named me president of the nurse's aide board. I held that position for years. After his death, his successor took a chance on me and allowed me to evangelize in a way that I've never thought. My trial sermon was on Wednesday, October 20, 2004 at 6:00 p.m.

This was during bible study in Melrose Park. The message was "The price you pay for a new life." I began to teach Sunday school and bible classes and I was also in charge of a prison ministry team. I was lead servant for the prison ministry. I facilitated the services at the women's prison at 26th and California. I was accompanied by a team of deacons and other female evangelists. On one particular visit, a sheriff brought in about 60 women.

The guards instructed them not to move out of their seats or they will be returned back to their cells.

The deacons began devotion. Afterwards I began to pray. I walked the floor and spoke to the hearts of the women. The women had created a choir while in prison. Ten of them offered to sing. I thought that it would be a great idea to include them into the program.

Beautiful notes hung in the air as the people clapped and sang along with them. Afterwards, I began to speak about life. I talked about why we go through trials. I talked about family and why we were even created.

Why were we created? God has a purpose for each and every one of us. We are created to give God glory. As I walked the floor I began speaking into the eyes and hearts of the women. I spoke to the hearts and Spirits of every person. All of a sudden women began to scream. It was as if pressure was being released from each of them.

They began to run and by the time I made it back to the front of the room, about 15 women were laying in front of the altar.

Some women were sobbing and others were lifting their hands. Some were on their knees with their hands raised in the surrender position. A few women were running laps around the room. The prison Chaplain remained in one spot.

The guards rushed into the room, their backs were against the 2 glass doors, but they did not move away from the doors. No one was escorted out of the room and no one was sent back to their cells. The prison Chaplain stated, "You can't keep the Holy Spirit inside of a box." These ladies needed a release! After about 20 minutes I did a benediction prayer. As the women began to collect themselves, they all began to line up. I stood at the door for hugs.

They ripped the corners off their bibles and wrote court dates and children's names on those ripped pieces of paper. Many whispered prayer requests in my ear. I prayed right there in silence each time out of fear that I may forget. The evangelists distributed care packages containing soaps, deodorant, toothbrushes and toothpaste, etc. This was truly a blessed service. I experienced another unexpected event.

My next door neighbor passed away. I went to the funeral along with my husband. The widow had asked me to read the obituary. I agreed to do it. While we were waiting for the service to start I sat behind the widow. My husband walked over to me and showed me the program. I said, "Yes I saw it." He went on to say, "No, look at the program closely." My name was printed next to the word, "Eulogy." I immediately stated to him that it was a misprint. The widow turned around and looked into my eyes. Without saying a word, I thought to myself, oh, God, I need your help. I was expected to speak.

I took my bible and read Psalms 91. After I read the entire verse, which was long, I dissected it. I used every verse and applied it to the life of the deceased. I spoke genuinely and from the heart. When the service was over, many family members and friends were very pleased and they all thanked me for a down-to-earth message. I had nothing to do with the outcome. It was all God.

YOUR TESTIMONY IS A
BLESSING FOR OTHERS

I consider Pastor Wheeler from Arkansas to be a Spiritual father and example to me. He sends me to hospitals on occasion to pray for the sick. Once, he called me and stated, "I am ordaining you spiritually." "You will run a spiritual clinic." I have to take notes when Pastor Wheeler calls because he is deep. I go and pray for every person that he ask. Miracles have happened.

When I was at my young daughter's book signing, Pastor Wheeler called me and said, "I felt you in my Spirit, what's going on?" I began to laugh as I told him how I was setting up at the library for the book signing. He goes out of his way to help so many people. If you can help somebody do it. Whatever your goal is in life, try your best and also help someone else along the way. We shouldn't want a goal if it requires stepping on some people to get it.

I was visiting my best friend's church and her pastor placed the microphone on a stand and sat it on the floor.

When I finished speaking the pastor assured me that God would reveal to me how many people that I blessed by my testimony. Your testimony is a blessing for others.

I went into the old neighborhood with an acquaintance. We attended Pastor Lane's service. I was praying near the altar during prayer time.

The Pastor stood me and my best friend's sister near his microphone. He instructed us to speak in tongues and do not stop until he told us. He said that he could hear chains falling off people. Normally I would refuse to speak in tongues in public. But when he asked, I did it. If somebody was getting deliverance and God is using us, then yes. My lips were moving but then, he yelled, "Out loud!" Now this was a service I will never forget.

My best friend Renee and I have known each other since the 3rd grade. That is a blessing. We are true friends. In most lifetimes we usually end up with one or two friends. Sometimes there are none. But I thank God for her friendship because she has my best interest at heart and prays more than anyone else that I know. I coordinated her wedding a few years ago. I was also blessed to stand as her matron of honor.

I can remember walking into my kindergarten class on the first day. A girl named "Desiree" walked over to me and showed me how to string beads. I attended a baby shower in

Minneapolis recently and got a chance to stop and visit Desiree. She still has that baby face. Old relationshipss are precious.

Wendy was my classmate from the 2nd grade. I was wondering what happened to her. A week and a half later, I went to my brother's class reunion with him and Wendy walked in with others.

She was also wondering whatever happened to me.

My mom and her best friend have been friends for over 60 years. I have been friends with my best friend over 40 years. A real friend keeps secrets. They support you. There is giving in friendship. There is laughter in friendship. Sometimes you may have to cry with them but tears are cleansing. A true friend prays with you.

Most people that you meet today are really acquaintances.

As a young child, my mother instructed us to call people "Associates." She didn't want us using the word "Friend" loosely. Some people are only co-workers, classmates or neighbors. But because you may have a conversation on occasion, some begin to believe that they are a friend. Have you ever thought someone was a good friend, but later they turned on you?

A real friend will stick closer than a brother. Some people are impossible to keep happy. Some are never satisfied. Some want you to constantly do for them, compliment them, run for them and they always have a sad story that drains you. They are energy suckers. It is not your responsibility to rescue anybody and you can't fix everyone's problem.

Becoming co-dependent means that you have allowed someone's problem to become your problem. Take a final look at that on-going drama and make a conscious decision to not take responsibility for anyone's happiness but your own.

We all have a story. The strong usually survives. The test is not just in the storm of life but it is in the survival. If you are going through a difficult time in your life; do not be confused by thinking that God is not there. If everything around you falls apart, you cannot. If you lose a loved one or friend, remember that if they were meant to stay they couldn't leave.

People are going to say and do things against your will. We cannot control their behavior. My daughter told me that she was at school and one classmate called the other a bad name. The one who was insulted began to cry. Some people feel injured as a result of people saying negative things.

But we have got to realize that we are not a victim of their words, but rather we are victims of how much power we give other people over our lives as a result of their words. I am not perfect. My system crashed before as a result of hearing negative words spoken about me. What I mean is, I literally got sick. That was a long time ago.

When you pray always ask for forgiveness first and then if there are attacks on your life, ask the Lord not to allow the enemy's attacks to have any power or authority over your life.

As we get older and wiser, we are renewed if we are listening and learning in the right environment.

My husband brought me a coat. Over time the back of the coat was damaged. I took the coat to Carson Pirie Scott furrier to have the back panel replaced. A few years later, I held up the coat and the new panel split away from the old part of the coat.

The power of the new skin broke away from the old skin. "You cannot put new wine in old bottles." The power of the new wine will burst the old bottles due to the weakness of the old bottle over time. Therefore, we must recreate the old bottle and put new wine in new skin. It is the same regarding our thinking. The mind has to be renewed.

Things change and people change. Some of us remember how we walked to the library to do research for school. In elementary school, if I forgot to research something, I walked all the way back to the library. Today, students can go online right inside of their own homes. There is nothing wrong with change. We do have to change for the better.

If you forget something today, it takes a click of a button to get more information. Someone came up with the idea of a "Bookless Public Library." It just opened in Texas. This is all-digital and the facility offers about 10,000 free e-books for the 1.7 million residents. We must make the changes that we want to see today. We must also get our advice from the right people.

MIX FAITH WITH THE WORD
OR IT WON'T WORK

We must hang around people who are go-getters. You can read the bible all day long and talk to the nicest people. I heard a pastor once say that if you do not mix faith with the Word it won't work. The bible defines faith as the substance of things hoped for and evidence of things not seen.

My husband often patrols our block on foot. Sometimes he gets together with about 5 other men on the block to walk the block. This usually happens when someone appears on our block loud, causing the residents to feel threatened. The men walk and talk to whoever is causing a disturbance. They protect their women and children.

One particular time, several neighbors contacted my husband about a building.

This building was abandoned and the door was swinging open. It sat on the end of our roll. It was an eye-sore for our block. The people said, "What if a body gets dumped inside of that building?" Others said that someone could get attacked or raped in the building.

I asked a few of the ladies on the block to pray with me about the building. My husband had gone to the alderman about this as well. We asked to have it pad locked. That never happened. We kept praying.

One day, a building a mile away collapsed. It was old and it just fell. No one was seriously hurt but a brick did hit one man in the leg.

Because this building fell, the mayor put out an order to have several buildings in the city razed. Can you guess which building was on that list? Yes, that building on our block was one of the buildings listed to be torn down.

They razed that building in one day and had the debris removed simultaneously. The lot is vacant. Thank you Lord. It took nearly a year but it happened.

I am moving into what I call my second phase in life. I am having a retirement celebration. Thirty years is a long time to work at one place. I am active and I love to travel. My mom would always suggest that a lady doesn't tell her age. But a woman who once worked in ministry with me said something. She said that her grandmother would say, "Tell your age when you age gracefully so that the young women will know that they don't have to dress provocatively." I was almost 40 when I gave birth to Jessica. We don't have to over accentuate the makeup to prove our value and worth. We must present ourselves with class and behave properly at all times. It is okay to have fun but we still must be ladies. The way that we behave matters so much. Have you ever heard someone say, "She looks like she's been around the block a few times?" Well, they are saying that they seem to have been with men intimately and often.

We don't want to be that person. I was at a funeral a while ago and I got a chance to talk to many people from the old neighborhood. When the service was about to begin, I sat down. Finally I heard, "Mary Sykes." "Sykes" was my maiden name.

I turned around and smiled. I said "Hello." The back row of the church was lined with men whom I had grown up with but I had not seen them in many years. It is so good to see old neighbors and acquaintances. It brought back memories.

One of the men saw me turn around after hearing my name. He said, "That's not the same 'Mary Sykes' that no one could touch?" Everyone laughed. Reputations follow us throughout life. There is always someone watching you. Not only are there always somebody watching you, we must be mindful about what we are watching. Many of the popular shows on television today depict single people with lead roles of "The other woman." The media paints this picture that it's okay to sleep around, cheat and be dishonest as long as you are pretty, clever, smart and know lots of famous people. The trickery will come back to you at one point or another. Back when I was younger a guy asked me for my number. I didn't know if it was okay to give him my number so I asked my mom would it be okay.

She said "Yes." I allowed the guy to come over to watch TV a few times.

Before I knew it he had spread all over school that we slept together. My brothers found out as well as others. Unfortunately, some neighborhood guys got a hold of him.

Almost the entire school turned on this guy, calling him a "Liar." No one believed him.

I was hurt and asked him never to call me again. He denied it but people that I knew and even those whom I was not familiar with attested to the fact that he indeed had spread the lie. One of my brothers had a friend who asked to meet me because of the outpour of support from my classmates.

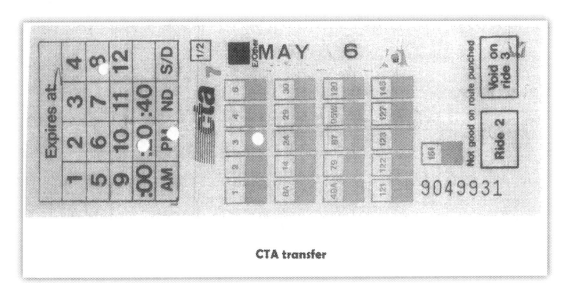

CTA transfer

He was like, "Wow, I'd like to meet your sister." My brother gave me the message but I declined the invitation because of the circumstances. I dated some very nice gentlemen. I went to movies or walks to the park.

I traveled by bus before on a date. You could board as many buses or trains that you would like within a matter of hours with a CTA transfer.

The super transfer pass was twenty cents on Sundays and lasted a full day. We went to see a movie, had dinner and walked around downtown. Many of the girls who bragged about how much a guy spent on them would usually be expected to give something back in return. Because a guy didn't have a car didn't mean the date wouldn't be a good one.

I dated a couple of guys fresh out of high school. I became very attached to one of the guy's mother. His mom taught me how to cook soul food.

She truly thought that I would be her daughter-in-law. One day he called and told me that he brought a car and that he would be driving on our next date. He picked me up holding 2 roses. He gave one to my mom and he gave one to me. The car looked fine. We went to Chi Chi's Mexican restaurant in Orland Park, Illinois. We arrived at the restaurant and he worked there as a cook. We sat down and he was introducing me to many of the staff.

I ordered Mexican style lasagna, French bread and salad.

I got unsweetened iced tea to drink. He ordered noodles. He then got me a souvenir chi chi's stuffed bear. I thanked him. We talked for a while at the table and he had a very interesting conversation as usual. After the date was over, he walked me to his car. It began to rain. I looked at my single rose but it began to turn dark in color. It had gotten a bit chilly outside so I asked him to please turn on the heat but he didn't. He started the car and I suggested he turn on his windshield wipers since it began to rain. He said, "I'd better get my pliers." He used these pliers to turn on the wipers, turn on the radio and let me out. I asked him, "Why don't you use those pliers to turn on some heat?"

He then stated that he didn't have heat. He said, "I got this baby for only one hundred bumps." What he meant was that he spent $100 for this car. He said that he got it for a real steal. I was thinking that they stole his one hundred dollars. I don't know anyone else who has enough nerve to drive such a car. It took him a while to get me back home because he kept jumping out of the car to wipe the windshield with a towel since the wipers eventually stopped working.

My big brother asked me about the date afterwards.

I described the date to him. My oldest brother is the type of person who laughs so hard that you need to get a cold towel and hold it to his face. I have dated some really nice people. I dated a couple of entertainment promoters. Because of this, I was able to go backstage during performances and meet many famous people. Many celebrities live a fast life. Fame has a dark side. Some would prefer that exciting life and others just want a quiet and simple life.

When I was a cheerleader in high school, if you were not dating the right type of guy, you didn't make the squad.

Your reputation mattered if you were going to lead cheers. I made the squad when I didn't have an official boyfriend. I did provide a clean reputation and my grades were good.

Cheerleading practice was at the same time as marching band rehearsals. I loved playing the flute and I received my music credits from band so I had to stop cheering on the field. I still cheered in the stands with my classmates. That was disappointing for me but I could not be in 2 places at one time. Life is full of disappointment yet it can also be filled with much joy.

LEAD WHEN IT IS NOT CONVENIENT

When something happens and it hurts; recognize it as an opportunity and not punishment. Some people prefer to pretend that certain things didn't happen. But, it is healthier to recognize it and don't try to do something to avoid feeling it. Feel every part of your situation and see what is there to teach you. Whatever comes your way, it is going to be alright.

Things are going to happen. People are going to come at you. People can be very disappointing. Lean back into your space and remember that you are not that trial that sits before you. "This too shall pass."

I have made some terrible mistakes in life. I learned from every one of them. I get many prayer requests and people can say and do some very mean and evil things to others.

One Sunday I was speaking to a group of young people and I had a terrible week. Everything that could go wrong did go wrong. I stood in front of that class and I took my mind off myself and my circumstances. Before I knew it the young people were laughing and even I felt better. I have taught 18 years.

Success is sharing who you are with others. Lead when it is not convenient. Be authentic and be a truthful leader. If it is your calling, you will be happy no matter what. I've never been on a church payroll.

I had a class to teach so I grabbed my bible and went to church. I usually tell my students when I don't feel good. I ask them to pray as I go along. This allows them to remember that I am human. Young people need us. They don't need to watch reality TV or explicit videos to get an image of how things should be for them.

I teach because I want to help as many people as I can. I also stretch out at home in prayer. I firmly believe that prayer is a secret weapon. I certainly need it.

There may be someone acting a complete fool around you. God may have His judgment already cut out for that person.

What if God is leaving you in that situation in order to see how long it takes for your heart to become humble towards people who act that way? Sometimes we get in our own way. Have you ever heard that saying, "They are messing with the wrong one?" Some people feel that they can handle an attack without help. That is why you see fist fights. You can use that type of person to help you purify your heart. Your enemies can bless your outcome. There is no blessing inside of a physical fight. I knew someone who kept yelling and cursing and died in the middle of a raging outburst. This person fell to the floor while cursing.

I also know of a lady in her 70s. She had a couple of strokes and a heart attack. One of her sons called her on the telephone in a panic. He was screaming "momma, Bernard got shot." Bernard is her youngest son. She was breathing slowly from the time she could hear her oldest son's voice. She remained calm and asked, "Oh, is he alright?" Her youngest son was alright and was taken to the hospital. But she spoke to him as if she was told that her son scrapped his knee. She was protecting her heart. She knew that she did everything she could for her children. Some prefer to live in a way that is displeasing to their parents. She knew that her children's lives are in God's hands. She accepted that truth.

There are people in life that you invest your time and money. As time evolves, they become mature, get jobs and are able to do better for themselves. Some will come back to you and let you know that they will never forget all that you've done for them. Then there are others who will act as if you've never done a thing for them simply because you stopped. Every deed that you've ever done for anyone, God was watching. You get your reward from God. If that person wants to celebrate you then that's a bonus.

There are riches in your experiences. It's not always about money. If you have a job, that is a reason to get to love more people. School is a reason to love more people. You get to nurture more souls.

When someone calls me in an excited voice, I calm myself immediately by taking a breath and then I ask, "What's happening?" If the other person is out of control; will freaking out help? It absolutely will not. I tell Jessica all of the time that there are two things that we cannot do anything about. Those two things are death and the weather. If someone betrays you, there is still room for growth. Think of the worst thing that ever happened to you. You got passed that moment of hurt because you are thinking back about it. Many times it's not the event where you suffered the hurt but the embarrassment of it all. There is no such thing as perfection. Well, only if you are talking about God.

I was watching an interview on television. Can you remember the "Dick Van Dyke Show"? Well, Dick had an assistant named "Buddy Sorrell." Buddy always had a joke and he was very funny. Buddy not only wrote comedy for this show, but he wrote for the best comedians back in the days. His real name was Morey Amsterdam. He is actually from Chicago. He also worked for Mr. Al Capone. After getting caught in gun fire, he moved to California. He was given the nickname, "The Human Joke Machine." Every time his mouth opened, a joke spilled out.

It is fair to say that he was a very happy man. Now, during this interview he made a statement. When asked, what is a life lesson that you've learned that you can tell the world? He said, "In everything that you do and everything that happens in life; there is always going to be that little bit of something that's not right."

How many of us can attest to that fact? This is a man that laughed more than anyone that I know in life. He understood this to be true and laughed anyway. I was complimenting someone. I told him that he was such a nice person and that he was generous. He is older and he said to me, "Mary, I am crazy." I hesitated and stared at him. He looked serious. There is an old saying, "When someone tells you who they are, believe them." I began watching him and sure enough, he was making things hard for others. I was at a church once in the suburbs. A woman's husband had just made a terrible scene in the middle of service and it caused the service to be interrupted. The wife buried her face inside of her hands and began to cry. The husband was escorted out of the sanctuary and no one went near the wife. She could not move. She just sat there sobbing. I went over there and put my arms around her. I sat with her until she had enough strength to get up. Her family had walked out. She gripped my hands so tightly. She wasn't really along; but shame depends on us buying into the belief that we are alone.

We've all had an embarrassing moment. Sometimes we cause it and sometimes others intentionally cause it on us. We all try hard to make it in this world. Life can disappoint us, but it is such a blessing. Each breath we take is a blessing. An 8 year old little boy called my mom recently. He asked my mom, "Is this hell?" She assured him that hell was a horrible place of outer darkness, weeping, moaning and gnashing of teeth. Mom told him that he had a home for refuge, shelter and a family. She told him that he still had his mom. Everything may not be perfect but he still gets to pray. In the earth he could still find peace. There are moments of disappointment but you have spaces that contain peace. My mom called me and said, "Now, here is an 8 year old wondering about this world." There is a spirit of murder and attack on our youth. Every day we watch the news and some innocent child gets shot or hurt. Our children are afraid to go outside to play. We can never pray too much for our youth.

If you are not yet where you want to be; God is forming you in the middle of the problem. Sometimes He has to push you all the way to the end.

If God allows a situation, He is simply filtering out your life. He is adding people to you or subtracting people from your life. Sometimes it's both. Trust that this will make you better.

We cause a vast majority of our own problems. The moment that chatter begins move away from it. Die to your old self and get a spiritual rebirth.

The minute that someone insults you, it is a test of your spirituality. It is not about what happened to you, it is about how you handled the matter. Now if you get angry, you give them your power. Getting caught up into retaliation is ego. At that moment of attack, move away from the wrong that's being done and find a loving way to keep your power.

If I think about attacking someone out of retaliation, I am blocking my own heart and causing much pain to myself.

Don't try to change others, change your mind about them. Give them to God. Love them anyway and move on. Now, in this state your heart is full of love and forgiveness. If your attacker attempts anything further it will not bother you because your heart is clean. Do you want to feel healed? Forgive somebody.

I apologize just in case I may have said something or did something. I clear the air. We don't have to hang around people who repeatedly practice iniquities. But get it right with people. There is no way to get a breakthrough in life holding on to hate. We cannot ask for things, get them and then stop praying either. That is called, "Asking amiss." Can God trust you with His secrets? Can He give you intercessory assignments? We should be able to help the people around us. God is not looking at what you are doing, He is focused on your heart and checking out the real you on the inside. If you hate people, He knows. God wants us to love people.

Have you ever said something, but later thought, "Perhaps I should have thought before I said or did that?" This is because we react first.

Now some people are programmed never to forget. Every time they see you, there's that look or they'll say something evil.

But if you can let go it is a higher calling. Now think about how many times God has delivered you. Whatever they've done, do not nurse the wounds. Don't sleep on it.

"Loose it and let it go." Is your level of chatter some gossip or a death threat? If you notice, you never get a straight path to your destination. There is always a bumpy road, twists and turns and road blocks. You stop and think about how perhaps you should never have started on your journey. It's dark and you can't see. You can't even find a detour. Don't retaliate, pray.

I was at another church. The pastor's dad approached me. He asked, "When it's dark outside, cloudy and grey, is the sun out?" I said, "No." He said, "Yes, it is you just can't see it." The SON is out but we just can't see HIM!

God puts desires at the level of our pain. Because of this, you gain the tenacity to try again.

It takes courage to be you. People will watch you pick out a watch and tell you, "Well, I don't like that watch." But if it's for you then you pick the watch. There is always mixed opinions about what you choose to do. Compare yourself against who God is and not people.

THIS EARTH IS FAITH SCHOOL

Many people don't believe that God is an incognito giver. They get things and have no clue of who gave the things to them. The bible tells us that "Every good and perfect gift comes from the Lord." Relationships are gifts. He is just not bragging and taking credit. If it hasn't been delivered yet, it is not time for the delivery. Some of our blessings are on back order. It's up to us.

Do you look at the souls of people or do you look at things from an outward appearance? Have you ever seen a person with everything but they can barely speak to people?

It takes a strong person to be humble. I often wonder if road rage is a split second decision to react to something that simply could have been avoided. An evil deed hurts the person that it was intended for and it also hurts the perpetrator.

Look at this earth as faith school. Practice faith every day. No human being can contribute to the growth and salvation process. God plants the increase. I once heard a minister say that a farmer can prepare the soil, plant the seed and water the seed. After the farmer has sweat, gotten dirty and tired, all he can do is go to sleep. God receives and allows it to grow. His harvest comes from God. All the farmer knows to do is go to sleep after a day's work.

But when that farmer lays his head down there is some faith attached to his belief system. I believe that there is no way anybody works that hard without some form of faith.

Plant your seed and desires. Wait and then go to sleep at night. Farmers go to bed at night and can't do anything but wait for the harvest. A farmer knows that he cannot grow crop. If he doesn't get enough sleep then he cannot plow the next morning. He allows God to do His part.

If you ever want to feel weightless, forgive everybody. Go positive on the negative. You cannot put a bandage on cancer. Drugs may bandage pain but it won't solve the problem. If life feels messy, it's not another person's fault. However, if someone attacked you and caused your life to now be limited, you have got to forgive. Move on for yourself. Whatever happened to you, get the right help in order to get rid of the pain.

You can cry yourself to death or move on. If someone is talking about you, let them talk. Work on controlling you and not other people. Winston Churchill once said, "A lie gets half way around the world before the truth has a chance to get its pants on." People love to spread words that make others feel low. The one who's spreading it thinks that they will look larger if they spread it. "See it's them not me." "They did this and I didn't." "It happened to them, it didn't happen to me." "See how high I sit when you compare me to them?"

A preacher once said, "Why don't you back yourself up against Jesus." Don't ever think that God does not love the homosexual because He does. Allow God to be the judge. "He that is without sin, let him cast the first stone." I love everybody. I must say that cross-dressing can get you killed. A friend asked me to stop by an elderly lady's home to check on her. We stopped to see if she needed anything. Her only son was in prison for murder. Her son picked up a date one night and woke up the next morning and found out that the person that he woke up to was actually a man. In a heated rage, he crushed his date's head with a hammer. He was fooled. But he also picked up a stranger and took that stranger home. The bible says, in Matthew 19, "Have ye not read, that HE which made them at the beginning made them male and female, and said, for this cause shall a man leave father and mother, and shall cleave to his wife: and they twain shall be one flesh? Wherefore they are no more two, but one flesh. What therefore God hath joined together, let not man put asunder." What God joins together, no man can divide.

I took a class called, "Religion in America". In this class I learned about different religions. We had guest who practiced various religions and I learned how they worshipped. This went on for weeks. At the beginning of this process I was frowning and in disbelief. Near the end of the experience, I learned to love each and every one of them.

Of course I talked about Jesus, but I also learned that a true spiritual being will love and never hate anybody.

Learn through love but also learn through pain. A religious person tries to control God but a Spiritual person always follows God. God is running the whole show. He is running your parents, your boss, your teacher, the pope, your pastor, your mate and everybody else.

It is not lonely at the top when we train someone and take them with us on this journey. We have got to train someone to take our place in the world. We must raise our children to build and not to take. Our children must be able to take care of themselves and not have to depend on others. Have you ever known a person who seems to behave out of control when they need money? My God brother puts it this way, "Some can't do broke." Before we had a fax machine inside of the house, I went to a currency exchange to fax a document. My mom was waiting in my car. The machine moved slowly and I was told that it would take about 10 minutes for a confirmation sheet to print. I walked next door to a well known grocery chain to get a ginger ale to drink for me and my mom. When I arrived back to the currency exchange I could not believe it. The man in the line next to me had 2 guns in his socks and tried to rob the currency exchange. My mom was sitting in the car watching them put this man in a squad car. She saw me walk next door.

No matter how messed up things seem to be, God will work it out for your good. The start of the matter is usually the hardest part. Real happy people do not have the best; they make the best out of whatever they've got. Remember that pot of chili my uncle made? It was made out of pork and beans. Today, I still remember that chili. I still remember how good it tasted and my brothers remember too. Love was mixed in that pot. Sometimes you have to "Make due."

In other words, take what you've got and do your best with it. Also, when we pray, we must make sure that it is God who is speaking to us. If you are trying to go up, get down first on your knees in order to get there. I remember a time when we needed extra help in the office. We needed help in order to catch up on a backlog of data entry. The supervisors hired 5 women from a temporary agency. I was given the task of making sure that they were issued a certain amount of cases each day; and I also had to make sure that we met a certain quota by the end of each day. These women exhibited a special natural ability and aptitude. They each was very hard-working and didn't mind staying to do overtime. They displayed a very successful work performance. They were talented. Finally the bosses gave them an assignment. They were given specific instructions to go down to a particular location and fill out paperwork.

They were asked to turn in a resume and other supporting documentation along with the application. They were offered full time, permanent positions. Four of the women did everything that was asked of them and one did not.

She did not go to the location to pick up the paperwork. She did not turn in her resume or anything else. She told us that the Lord wanted her to stand still and do nothing. She said to us that she would be hired regardless. She felt that she didn't have to fill out all of those papers. She was already hired by the temp agency. The four women who turned in everything settled their accounts with the bosses and were hired full time, permanently with full benefits. The one servant who did nothing to allow her career to grow ended up losing her position. Later, when she needed a reference or any other help, I helped her. This reminds me of the story in the bible about the talents. The master gave 3 of his servant's talents of gold. To the first servant the master gave five talents, and to the second servant he gave 2 talents. But to the third servant the master gave only 1 talent of gold. The first servant doubled his five totaling ten talents. The second servant doubled his 2 totaling four talents. The master entrusted them to use the talents and they gained more.

But the third servant who was only given 1 talent was really afraid and went out and hid the gold in the ground. When the master returned, the third servant still had the same talent that was given to him. He had buried it. The master replied, "You wicked, lazy servant." The master took the bag of gold from him and gave it to the first servant who started off with five talents and doubled them to ten. Sometimes we miss the mark unknowingly. Fear has caused me to mess up many times. God is still a God of a second chance. The worker who did nothing had a real dream. She really wanted to raise foster children. Every time she attempted to get foster children something got in the way. One day her sister passed away and she ended up raising her own blood relatives. Her sister's children became her children. God knew she would have custody of her family back when the bosses asked for that paperwork.

I pray that none of us pass up unnecessary blessings because we feel that we are doing the right thing.

We all make mistakes and we've all messed up at one time or another. God loves the sinner but He judges sin. If I try to judge someone today, I've just told everybody exactly who I am.

If God gives you a powerful position, please do not use that position to mistreat people just because you have that power. God is no respecter of persons.

He loves all of us. Sometimes you may hear someone in trouble say, "Something kept telling me to do it." They caused harm to another person because they listen to something on the inside of them. The person who you think is the enemy is not the real enemy. The real enemy works behind the scenes. Cancers and sickness is just a front. Something is causing these things to happen.

When that doctor told me that I was dying, I had to defend my life by telling her, "No, I am not." I could have accepted that but I didn't. Speak positive things out of your mouth and shift the atmosphere. We cannot think wrong and live right. When the enemy tries to invade your thoughts don't let the enemy win. When you store a lot of money in your bank account, you have security and you are well established. You won't worry. Store up some prayers in order to build up your account in heaven.

When you do this, God hears you talking to Him and He can check your account when you come asking for help! He sees that you are well established.

A woman called me once and told me about a horrible dream that she had about me. The dream didn't upset me as much as the fact that she was laughing about what happened in her dream.

I listened but I try to never put my mouth against people. The horrible and vicious dream turned out to be about her. It was tragic and it is truly hard to talk about.

Putting our mouths on people is dangerous. We cannot afford to have our past in front of us. Our past should be behind us. Love people and pray. If you don't know what to pray, ask God to work against emotions. Ask Him to bless your mind, health, family, children, finances, community, church, and your future. Ask in the name of Jesus.

Don't fight in the natural with negative words and fist fights. Shut the door and go into prayer. Ask God to hit a supernatural delete button from bad situations and bad memory.

Pray like never before, fast like never before and be careful with whom you share your plans. Your actions and conversation are your only faith. Your tongue is spoken faith. You need the faith for what you are trying to gain.

I have been with my husband for quite some time now. If you are in a marriage covenant; it's only because you both want it. It is impossible to have a real relationship when only one mate wants it. Both parties have to want it in order for it to work.

MARRIAGE: LOVE YOUR MATE

Right before my wedding, a man told me that it is very easy to take advantage inside of marriage. Communicating with each other is very important. If your spouse has said or done something, you must confront the issue. Don't wait, put it right there on the table. Discuss your likes and dislikes.

Repeating of Wedding Vows
Lake Geneva, WI
Garden Theme Wedding & Dinner

TITUS & MARY

My late pastor Mosley counseled us in his chambers for an hour right before our wedding. He was proud of us. A week later, my husband's pastor, H. McNelty and his wife counseled us in their home.

They spent 4 hours with us. We discussed marriage and the family. After the meeting, they moved our wedding date to July 19, 1997. They were old fashioned and stated that the engagement was too long. We didn't think 10 months was long.

One thing that I will never forget is when they told us that someone was going to come to each of us and say that they saw the other talking and getting too acquainted with the opposite sex. They assured us that someone would lie and allow the devil to use them. Pastor was right.

They said that marriage was the best relationship in the world. They finished our session by stating that I would make a beautiful wife for Titus. I admired them so much. Titus proposed to me in front of my family during Thanksgiving dinner.

Afterwards, we drove to Hillside, Illinois and he proposed to me again in front of his side of the family during their Thanksgiving dinner. This was a very exciting time for us. My husband picked up me and his sister. He took us to Whitehall jewelers at North Riverside to select my wedding ring. I am still wearing the ring I fell in love with and no upgrades on my ring. Titus worked overtime and sweat for my ring. It is 10 feet tall. We were married the following summer. We both wanted a church wedding.

My husband purchased us a home. Neither of us had bills. He carried me across the threshold in my Ivory wedding gown on our wedding night. Right after our reception, we went straight to our new home. We were so excited about the house that we didn't want to leave.

We drove to Gurnee, Illinois the following weekend. We shopped, had dinner and spent the weekend in Gurnee. We really didn't take our actual distant honeymoon until 8 months later. We went to Jamaica for 8 days. We stayed in Montego Bay, and spent a day in Negril and another day in Ocho Rios. We had a great time. The bible tells us that once you are married, two become one flesh. You are one flesh. His family becomes yours and her family becomes his family. Whatever he possesses is hers and whatever she possesses is his possession. The bible is not a lie. You each gain more family. If your relationship is good with your family, may God continue to richly bless you. If it's cold and distant, keep praying. Never think that you don't have a relationship.

You have one if you are married. It may be distant but that is your family. Love your family and never stop praying. I went to college with a young lady who shared a story with me. She said that her in-laws asked her to come over for Thanksgiving dinner. She said that they wanted to know her favorite part of the turkey. She told them that she loved the legs and wings on the turkey. She then went on to say how excited she was to visit her in-law's home for the holidays.

She said that she could not wait to sit down with them to eat. To her amazement, she entered the dining area of the house and saw a big turkey at the center of the table. She said, "I was looking at a big turkey with no legs and wings!" Instead of not inviting her, they decided to personally invite her but include an insult. Some family will not invite certain members over at all. When family members decide not to share; they miss out on special times, unique events, love and laughter with family.

Let God be the judge and love people. If it is safe and more peaceful to stay home and not visit, then stay home. Let your prayers be yes and amen. God is not the author of confusion. Marriage is not a right but a privilege. The union cannot be taken lightly. If someone doesn't like your spouse, they don't like you either. The two of you are one.

Another college classmate shared an experience.

She said that her fiancée took her away for the weekend to officially propose. Her ring was breath-taking. She said that when she arrived into her suite there were 3 gifts. One was a huge arrangement of flowers from her soon-to-be husband. The second gift was assorted cheese from her future mother-in-law and the third gift was a basket from her entire in-law family. There were cards expressing "Welcome to the family." They showered so much love on her that she could not help but to be humble. They knew just how much her fiancée loved her.

When do you know you are in love? Can you look at them and it's like looking in a mirror? Do you compliment each other? Do you love spending time together? Do you feel as though you cannot make it without them? It is lust when all a person wants is one thing and doesn't care about anything else. Human desires are intimately connected to one another. There is a right way and a wrong way. We have got to spend our time wisely. My husband did a lot of overtime at work when we first got married. He still does but I had to get use to it. I can remember going to a church on Friday nights in the neighborhood. I knew that Titus would be working late, so I would drive over to hear some good preaching and singing. Juanita Bynum would minister along with others. Gospel recording artist Kim Stratton would sing.

Now I could sit front and center. The service was free and I always had a good evening. This was a positive way to spend my free time.

It was gossip free and my mind was emotionally clear. This caused my home to be emotionally clear to receive my husband when he arrived home from work.

Does trauma bring married couples closer or not? I would have to say that it depends on the couple. We are not free to run away from trauma in marriage. Now if you are being beaten then yes. If you are having disagreements, that happens. The minister said, "For better or for worst"

during the wedding ceremony. You heard that. You said, "I do."

You got your marriage license and walked away with God's covenant in your spirit and went home. My husband and I were both raised in two totally different households. His family put the toilet tissue roll over. My family put the toilet tissue roll under. You come to a mutual agreement and keep it moving. Every day is an opportunity. My husband and I have date nights and movie nights. We send loving text messages. We kiss each other daily. If we have disappointing words, we talk and put all feelings out in the open. It gets quiet for hours sometimes.

Eventually one of us will say, "Hey, do you want to watch a movie?" The mess is not more important than us. Every moment is a gift. We do not have the perfect marriage because that doesn't exist. God wants marriage to be successful. So many people quote the bible where it says, "Wives submit yourselves to your own husband. "Husbands, love your wives, even as Christ also loved the church." But right before these verses, it also says "Submitting yourselves one to another." That is in the book of Ephesians. Everybody needs to submit. When everyone is loved and being treated with equal respect you will experience good results. If everyone is full of love without dictating all of the time, it's like heaven on earth.

If we ask God to lead our homes, He will make decisions for us. My husband is good with numbers and he was a banker for many years. Currently he is at the job of his choice because he continuously claimed it. One day he passed the test and got promoted. He said, "I am getting that job!" One day he called me from work with the news and all I could say was, "Wow, you claimed it."

The man guides and directs all matters in the household and he is a provider and protector of his family.

Marriage is built on faithfulness, trust, loyalty and a mutual love of God.

If any of these qualities are missing, keep praying! You truly find out about people once you live with them. 1 Corinthians 7 tells us that an unbelieving spouse is sanctified through the believing spouse. Where ever your spouse is lacking in the Word; share it with them. Equally yoked Christian couples both study and read the Word. They both believe in the Lord and each other 100 percent.

I was watching television and there was a couple on who had been married 75 years. When asked about the secret to their long-lasting marriage, the husband clearly stated, "Just forget about it". He and his wife both agreed that when disagreements occur, let it go. The mess is not more important than the two of you. They left confusion behind each day. They certainly looked happy to me. 75 years was a long time. Obviously they knew something that we don't.

The Word of God has to be the final authority in all matters. Love grows when each of you see the Lord more inside of each other. If you are single it works when you express total contentment within yourself and develop patience to wait on God.

Our children must be surrendered to the Lord and we must trust God and raise them in the fear of the Lord. Women are sensitive and we got that honest.

In the bible, the book of Genesis talks about sorrows being increased in women. Women are emotional. It is innate. We are receivers. Our bodies are even designed to receive. Women love very hard. We nurture our children and love our man. Women cook, clean, wash and meet the needs in our homes. Women are priceless. Her "Merchandise is good."

Men are expected to be this huge tower of strength. They are not allowed to cry without being called a punk. That's a trap to me. I think that everyone should be able to release pressure when it is time. If we can't open something, we look to men.

If we cannot lift something we look to men. Some men are challenged simply by attempting to drive or cross the street. We should never make our men feel trapped. When he comes home, he should have the best time ever.

His home should be his place of peace. We can never react to a single comment. We cannot reduce comments to a single moment. Some messed up relationships could be because people despise themselves.

If I cannot love myself, I cannot love you.

Pieces of yourself won't work. You have to give your all. Embrace yourself in your mate. Relaxing and engaging into quiet, intimate conversations mean so much. I try to always acknowledge the present and not last year. This took me some practice. Even if something current reminds you of last year, you still must leave old stuff in the past.

If God says that you are one, whoever makes a bad statement about your spouse just said it about you. What others think about your spouse is none of your business. Right before purchasing our house, my husband would take me to the lake front and we would talk about our wedding plans. We talked about the church. We talked about our family.

We would rush after work because we knew that we would meet and hang out somewhere to discuss our future. We would park in front of the home we now live in and talk about raising children. We talked about who probably lived in the house at the time. We parked in front of the house so many times that the minister who was house-sitting finally came to the door and motioned for us to come inside. We walked into the house which was our second time.

It was completely empty except for the room that the minister used for sleeping. He had fixed a small area of comfort for himself. He had a white bible in the empty living room.

He showed us the house a second time and then held our hands and prayed with us.

He said that he would be in prayer about us getting the house. He said that everyone that looked at this particular home loved it. When we got the call that my husband had actually been approved for the home, we jumped for joy. The home was completely rehabbed and looked completely new. No work had to be done accept for the basement. It was unfinished. My husband hired a crew and allowed me to draw the plans on the layout of our new basement.

TITUS & MARY BANKS
WEDDING-JULY 19, 1997

I was excited and that made me feel good. I drew a family room, laundry room, small kitchen area, extra bedroom and closet space. It turned out really nice and we were both pleased.

The very first time we turned the key and entered the house as owners felt good. The white bible that the minister kept in the living room was lying there as a gift to us. While dating we would get on our knees together and pray. We still pray together today.

"A cord of 3 strands is not easily broken." That means that when you include the Lord in your marriage, it's not easy for the yoke to break.

I mentioned before that we waited nearly five years to have Jessica. We travelled a lot.

Jessica is a promised child that the book of Genesis talks about. Her heart was once inside of me.

Pregnant women travel with two beating hearts. Only God can allow that to happen.

Would you purposely feed your new born baby poison? Some of us do without even realizing it. If your heart is full of resentment, evil and un-forgiveness, that's poison. That poison will pass on to your unborn child. We must free our mind, body, heart and spirits from anything that is unclean.

During my pregnancy I read scriptures, meditated and loved people. I ran from filthy words. My daughter Jessica came out loving everyone. I fed her an instant-formula called "Love." She was born with a belly full of love. If you belong to a church, your church may have a vision statement. It is a description of the direction your church is going. Do a vision statement over your life. Plan your life's goals. Believe in your dreams and make them happen.

If you want something better in life then go for it. Take a deep breath with the breath that God gave you and do it. Be happy with yourself. It's not about money or popularity. Once you stop feeling scared, you can do anything you desire. Your desires won't mean anything to God or others until they mean everything to you. We all have a history.

PREGNANT WOMEN TRAVEL WITH TWO HEARTS

Step away from that and move forward. Every hurtful thing that ever happened to you shaped you into the person you are right now.

Try not to keep negative items and reminders in your home. If you have a letter or card that makes you sad shred it. Prayer is the vehicle that we need to carry out our blessings.

Let's stop giving the flesh all of these gifts since it is turning into dust eventually. God is our adjuster. We move and adjust into new and exciting changes. Sometimes adjustment hurts. Things are moving around and changing.

There are all types of signs when you are around people. Be honest and love yourself. When you love you, others will too. Do your best in life and make your future happen. If you want to start a business then do it.

If you have an unusual idea, explore your dreams. Remember when I mentioned the new bookless digital library? If the person who just started that library was afraid, we'd never know anything about having a digital library. Somebody has got to do it so why not you?

Whatever your purpose is in life, God can use you. The only one who truly gets the credit is God. You get the benefits. If you want to put a stop to your own blessings, then start taking credit. Surrender completely to Him. Start off with a clean heart.

MEET A REAL MAN

Terrible things happen to unbelievers who sin, but God can transform that life. Your words can be more explosive than the atomic bomb. You can use them to destroy life or build up people.

Right where you are, God says that He will never leave you or forsake you. That means that He is living inside of you. That is a promise from God Himself.

There are 66 books in the Holy Bible. There are a total of 1188 chapters in the bible. The center of the bible is Psalm 118. That means that there are 594 chapters before Psalm 118 and 594 chapters after Psalm 118.

The very center verse is Psalm 118:8 "It is better to trust in the Lord than to put confidence in man." Keep this verse in the center of your heart.

The devil has been losing for a very long time. After you finish with all of this work down here, you get to have eternal life!

When you have faith, you are not exempt from obstacles. Faith moves you through your problems and gets you pass troubles. You are not outside of the trouble zone, you simply have some help. You are not going to make it without Jesus.

If you don't know who that is, let me introduce Him. He was conceived by the Holy Spirit. He led a sinless life.

He took on all of our sins. He died, but then rose again. He is seated at the right hand of God the Father.

Men are lost and are at the judgment of Christ. He is the one who has all power in His hands. He is a wonderful counselor. He is a mighty God. He is a Prince of peace. He is a Savior.

Oh, I know a man. He's not the cable man either but He is jealous. He doesn't want you winking at no other God but Him. His name is Jesus. He is the author and finisher of our faith. You are not going to get there without Him. Do you want peace in your home? Ask Him for help.

Get to know Him for yourself. Include Him in everything that you do. That is how we will have a successful, peaceable life filled with relationships and love with everyone.

ABOUT THE AUTHOR

MARY ELAINE BANKS is a Christian. She is a bible scholar studying divinity. She is also a prayer warrior. She knows that success is sharing who you are with others.

Mary's mission is to tell people that God loves them and to remind them just who they are in Christ. She wants people to know that the only faith that we have is our actions and our conversation. Our desires won't mean anything to God or other people until they mean everything to us.

She has taught bible classes for 18 years and discusses the application to daily living. In her writing she compels people to make the best out of whatever you've got. She stresses that a true spiritual being will love and never hate anyone.

Mary accepted the lord as her personal Savior as a young girl. She has been called to teach and evangelize about the Word of God. As a part of her mandate, she travels to hospitals on intercessory prayer missions. She is also a notary public making house calls to the sick and shut in.

Mary has a bachelor's degree in communications from DePaul University. She also has a master's degree in biblical studies. She has associates in Stenography and Legal secretarial science.

Mary spent 30 years working in law enforcement administration while also serving voluntarily in various capacities in the local church. She works diligently in her community as secretary of her block club alongside her husband who is the president. She is a parent volunteer at her daughter's school as well as in the community.

Mary enjoys writing and traveling. Her favorite exercise is walking and jogging. She wants everyone to know that difficult situations must be examined; because it is healthy to recognize it without avoidance. In her book, she explains that some of our problems may be there for a very long time in order to teach us; and to see how long it takes our hearts to become humble. She has taught her students to be the change that they want to see in the world.

She resides in Illinois with her husband Titus and 13 year old daughter Jessica. She also has 2 adult children, Titus Jr. and Kiehla.

Printed in the United States
By Bookmasters